Praise for *The Marie Laveau*

T0032138

"*The Marie Laveau Voodoo Grimoire* is a powerful addition to Denise Alvarado's previous works on New Orleans's history and Mam'zelle's legacy. The book is both practical and inspiring. It contains information and instructions that provide the reader with practical steps to incorporate the rituals, rites, and recipes of Laveau Voodoo into their daily life. Pay special attention to the herbal charts, the list of oils and perfumes, shells, stones, and other materials that can be used effectively by people at varying levels of experience. The Conjure in the Kitchen chapter provides recipes that are perfect for the Ancestral Feasts held by people of many traditions. This book is inspiring. Mam'zelle Marie and the legacy of Voodoo have often been maligned by mainstream media and treated with cockeyed reporting from well-meaning apologists. Denise has done the research needed to tell the whole story. She portrays the life and works of Mam'zelle with respect, understanding, and emotional sensitivity. It reads well as the history of a community of humans led by the influence of powerful and compassionate women.

Sit back, read, gather your altar items, and prepare to conjure your best life. Power forward."

—Yeye Luisah Teish, author of *Jambalaya: The Natural Woman's Book of Personal Charms and Practical Rituals* and *A Calabash of Cowries: Ancient Wisdom for Modern Times*

"*The Marie Laveau Voodoo Grimoire* is the stuff! Everything about this book feels just right. It's spare yet lush; vintage but with a fresh tone. Like Grandma's dresser, it's filled with sensual delights and well-kept secrets. I was hooked from page one. I want this book. I need this book in my magickal library, and you will too. Sister, you had me at Potlikker!"

—Priestess Stephanie Rose Bird, magick-maker, artist, and author of *Motherland Herbal* and *African American Magick*

"*The Marie Laveau Voodoo Grimoire* is, without a doubt, the most delightful book I've read this year! Offering a glimpse into Marie Laveau's life via historical tidbits, newspaper clippings, and quotations from those who knew her, this book is anything but a typical grimoire. While you'll find the anticipated fare of charms, spells, formulas, and rituals, there's also the unexpected surprise of recipes for bath and beauty, laundry and cleaning products, cures and remedies for minor afflictions, and—my personal favorite—traditional Southern dishes to prepare for family and friends. What Denise Alvarado has given us with this book is much more than a simple grimoire. It's a rare gift—a quintessential guide to conjuring a magical life—and one that all practitioners will use and cherish."

—Dorothy Morrison, author of *Utterly Wicked*

"*The Marie Laveau Voodoo Grimoire* is a compelling exploration of Voodoo traditions, dispelling myths and offering deep insights into the spiritual practices of this ancient and misunderstood religion. Denise Alvarado's writing is both engaging and informative, making it accessible to both newcomers and seasoned practitioners alike. Whether you are a curious reader interested in the occult or a dedicated student of Voodoo, this book provides a rich and enlightening experience. Once again her impeccably researched material offers her readers much more than expected."

—Denise Augustine, owner of Our Sacred Stories Tour Company

"To quote Denise Alvarado, 'a book has the power to bewitch and enchant,' and *The Marie Laveau Voodoo Grimoire* certainly fulfills that potential. Denise evokes the atmosphere of Maire Laveau's New Orleans: its bayous, swamps, moods, and mysteries. The book's themes are carried from ancient sources through Marie Laveau's day into our times. Voodoo's long history snakes through the contributions of many root workers, including the mighty Marie Laveau. Voodoo morphs, adapts and transforms as it weaves through time, experience, and changing circumstances. Alvarado's work is thorough, respectful, and rooted in her own deep knowledge of traditional practices, coupled with an anthropologist's attention to meticulous research. At the same time, she is unafraid to interpret and expand to reflect contemporary needs as well as her own inspiration. *The Marie Laveau Voodoo Grimoire* is full of useful information. But this is not a simple recipe book. The author explores the why's and wherefores—why you might want to employ a certain ingredient, what the meaning and power is within the ingredient, as well as the metaphor of the particular spell that renders the work effective. The author pays respect to and acknowledges the many practitioners who contributed spells and recipes. She doesn't claim to have discovered Marie Laveau's secret grimoire. Rather, by building creatively upon tradition, Denise Alvarado embodies the spirit of Marie Laveau, which elevates the work and lends vibrancy to her great legacy."

—Sallie Ann Glassman, author of *Vodou Visions*, artist and cocreator of *The New Orleans Voodoo Tarot*

"*The Marie Laveau Voodoo Grimoire* by Denise Alvarado is a book steeped in New Orleans mysticism. It is a foundational understanding of Voodoo rites and rituals that delve way beyond the lore and fascination with Laveau's enchanting hold on the city. This book is a must-have for folks researching the residual impact of spirituality on displaced Africans who call New Orleans family. Alvarado has written a prolific and redemptive tale, a delicious stew of just how revolution got its claim to fame."

—Mawiyah Kai El-Jamah Bomani, author of *Conjuring the Calabash: Empowering Women with Hoodoo Spells and Magick*

"Denise Alvarado is the most impressive, dedicated author on all things New Orleans Voodoo I can name. Her research is always impeccable; her love of the practice apparent from the first page of any of her books. And perhaps no historical New Orleans Voodoo personality has captured the fascination of devotees of the spirituality and lovers of New Orleans history alike than Marie Laveau. When I learned Denise was researching and compiling a grimoire of Ms. Laveau's recipes, I was thrilled. *This* would prove to be a truly trustable text, as are all of Alvarado's books. Moreover, her writing style is so accessible and clear, it promises to be a collection we can all use and which will remain in use well into the future. I attempted to put together a valid collection of Marie Laveau's practical work in magick for years. I know the effort, patience, and passion required to put this book together. Including myself, I can think of no New Orleans Voodoo authority and author better equipped to bring this information to the public. I am beyond excited about *The Marie Laveau Voodoo Grimoire* (and maybe a little jealous). Congratulations, Denise!"

—Claudia Williams, author of *Manifesting Magick with Vévés and Sigils* and other books, owner of Starling Magickal Occult Shop in New Orleans

The

MARIE LAVEAU

VOODOO

GRIMOIRE

The

MARIE LAVEAU
VOODOO
GRIMOIRE

Rituals, Recipes, and Spells for Healing, Protection, Beauty, Love, and More

DENISE ALVARADO

WEISER BOOKS

This edition first published in 2024 by Weiser Books, an imprint of

Red Wheel/Weiser, LLC
With offices at:
65 Parker Street, Suite 7
Newburyport, MA 01950
www.redwheelweiser.com

ISBN: 978-1-57863-813-0
Library of Congress Cataloging-in-Publication Data available upon request.

Cover design by Sky Peck Design
Interior by Debby Dutton
Typeset in Adobe Garamond and Frutiger LT

Printed in the United States of America
IBI
10 9 8 7 6 5 4 3 2 1

NOTE: This book contains advice, information, spells, and other remedies relating to plants and herbs and is not meant to diagnose, treat, or prescribe. It should be used to supplement, not replace, the advice of your physician or other trained healthcare practitioner. If you know or suspect you have a medical condition, are experiencing physical symptoms, or if you feel unwell, seek your physician's advice before embarking on any medical program or treatment. The spells and rituals in this book are for information only and should not be practiced by anyone without proper training. The author and publisher are not responsible if the recipes and spells do not have the desired effect or if adverse effects are caused. Readers using the information in this book do so entirely at their own risk, and the author and publisher accept no liability if adverse effects are caused.

To Brandon
The legacy is now yours

Silence, my soul, Goddess is here.

CONTENTS

INTRODUCTION

Marie Laveau was one of the wisest women that ever lived. She was gifted with a power from on high that very few people are gifted with. She could look at you without ever having seen you before and tell you where you were born, what hour you were born and the time, and also the condition of the weather if you wanted to know that. She was, in a way, to me another Solomon, sent from the Almighty God above to come down here and help his people. I also picture her as a John De Baptist who comes to teach right and righteousness. This woman I am telling you about prayed not three times a day as Daniel did but prayed every hour in the day that our Heavenly Father sent. I picture her as one chosen by God's own hand. She was not selfish but waited on the black as well as the white and the rich as well as the poor. Doing all the good stuff she could. And never doing any harm to anybody.

—Old Man George Nelson, 1936

"Shut that goddamn door!" exclaimed the Voudou Queen when the police showed up to raid another of her ceremonies. Marie Laveau didn't have time for the nonsense that was ensuing. She was used to it, sure, and she was not incarcerated herself, but it cost her time and money, nonetheless. She advocated for women needing a voice in the courtrooms and saved the condemned from the gallows on more than one occasion. She bailed out folks who needed it and gris grised the judges, attorneys, and police chiefs to respond in her favor. And if they didn't, she had ways of reminding them it's not a good idea to cross the Voudou Queen. A particular segment, however, reveled in harassing the Voudous and enforcing the laws. Voudou was illegal, after all. And the people either loved, feared, or hated Marie Laveau. Even so, many joined her ritual activities on the downlow. They wanted to know her secrets, like how to dance publicly with wild abandon while simultaneously being a devout Catholic. Who was this boss woman of the 1800s? How did she garner so much power? Her influence over the people in the city was undeniable.

Marie Laveau was a free Creole woman of color living in nineteenth-century New Orleans who became famous as a Voudou Queen.[1] She is known for her entrepreneurial savvy and is credited for making a business out of Voudou[2] and Hoodoo.[3] She was known in all sectors of the city, having significant connections in the legal system and the Catholic Church. But Voudou is not the only thing Marie Laveau is known for. She is most loved and remembered by New Orleanians for her charity work, prison ministry, and service to the community. Nonetheless, she was often targeted and harassed by the police. The press covered the raids on the Voudous and their subsequent court appearances with a salacious slant whenever possible. Despite having a target on her back, however, police officers, lawyers, and judges were regular attendees at her annual St. John's Eve dances. And one of her boyfriends, after the death of her partner, Christophe Glapion, was rumored to have been an influential white lawyer.

Marie had nine children—two with her first husband, Jacques Paris, and seven with her common-law husband, Christophe Glapion. It is unknown what became of her children with Paris, as he apparently disappeared without a trace, possibly with them. New evidence suggests that Jacques Paris did not die until 1823 and that he lived in Baton Rouge, Louisiana, for some time, possibly for work. He was buried in an unmarked grave in St. Joseph Catholic Cemetery in Baton Rouge. Only two of Marie's children with Christophe Glapion survived until adulthood: Marie Eucharist Eloise Laveau, and Marie Philomène Glapion. According to legend, Marie Philomene became her mother's successor in the world of New Orleans Voudou and is known as Marie Laveau II.[4]

At any given time, Marie Laveau could be found in dark, steam-filled rooms around the city, where she tended to those afflicted with deadly diseases such as cholera and yellow fever. Yet she did not contract the diseases herself. Whereas the average life expectancy at that time was just over thirty years, Marie Laveau lived to the ripe old age of nearly eighty! It says a lot about her lifestyle and resiliency to live that long. Her uncharacteristic longevity also explains the rumors that she was immortal and that her daughter took on her identity after her death, giving the appearance of a supernaturally long life. In fact, there is no substantial evidence that either of her daughters carried on her Voudou activities upon her retirement or death. It appears she was simply blessed with a long and fruitful life.

In my book *The Magic of Marie Laveau*, I documented a specific tradition that emerged from Louisiana Voodoo that I call Laveau Voudou. A variation of New Orleans Voudou, Laveau Voudou is the style of Louisiana Voudou practiced by Marie Laveau. It looks a lot like what folks nowadays call Hoodoo, but it has a distinctly Catholic flavor with a touch of performance art for good measure. Candles, incense, baptisms, holy water, crucifixes, altars, flowers, and petitioning the saints are found in both Catholic rites and Marie Laveau's Voudou rituals. But to understand Laveau Voudou and, therefore, the contents of this grimoire, we must first cover some basic concepts about Louisiana Voudou.

LOUISIANA VOODOO

Louisiana Voodoo is the umbrella term for several forms of Voudou in Louisiana. It refers to a folk religion more likely to be practiced by individuals or families than by communities. The most well-known form of Voudou in Louisiana is New Orleans Voudou. The communal aspect of Voudou is observed in New Orleans, where public ceremonies, dances, drum circles, baptisms, and other events occur. New Orleans is where a concentration of practitioners reside, and where a thriving tourist trade exists, so there are publicly known Voudou houses and temples. I suspect just as many or even more practitioners remain underground. They prefer to stay out of the public eye due to the stigma attached to Voudou and the safety issues that can arise when a person is known to be a Voudouist.

A young religion that emerged from the transatlantic slave trade, New Orleans Voudou developed throughout the eighteenth, nineteenth, and twentieth centuries in Louisiana. Its foundational structure is identical to West African Vodun in important ways. It is a matriarchal tradition whereby women dominate the clergy. And though it may be the wild child of the African Vodun, it is no less legitimate or complex.

West African Vodun cosmology centers around spirits and divine energies that govern the earth. These energies and spirits are called *vodun*, meaning "spirit." They govern nature and humanity and consist of major deities, from a sky pantheon of thunder, lightning, and rain; to the water spirits who dwell in lakes, rivers, and the sea; to nature spirits associated with rocks, hills, wind, animals, and trees. In New Orleans Voudou, the vodun are referred to as spirits. These spirits exist on a hierarchy of three levels: At the top is *Bon Dieu* (Good God). Below are powerful intermediary spirits known as loas, orishas, and the ancestors. Third, saints, angels, spirit guides, regional and familial spirits, and revered cultural heroes are acknowledged. Ancestor reverence is the most important aspect of all forms of Voudou. The loas, orishas, and ancestors are not worshipped; rather, they are served and revered, respectively.[5]

New Orleans Voudou is a religious system that acknowledges the existence of one ultimate God while not denying the existence of other deities.[6] Bon Dieu exists in theory, but in practical terms he is distant from humans and does not interact with us:

> God is too busy to listen to the pleas of men, so the loas and the Saints meet at the halfway point on the road between Heaven and earth, and the loas tell "their brothers" what their human followers want. The Saints then return to God and report on the appeals which men have made to the loas, and God grants or refuses the various requests.[7]

This hierarchical structure demonstrates the importance of the spirits of Voudou. They function in a similar fashion to the Catholic saints as messengers to God, each holding an area of expertise, as it were, and can be petitioned for special favors.

New Orleans Voudou and Hoodoo are closely related. In Marie Laveau's day, the two traditions were essentially one and the same. Today, many practitioners of one also practice the other. Hoodoo, Conjure, and Rootwork—all terms used in this grimoire—are folk magick traditions that grew from the same conditions as Voudou. The terms Hoodoo and Conjure are often used interchangeably. On the other hand, Rootwork is a type of Conjure that uses plants for magickal work and healing cures. Each tradition is a resistance response to the harsh realities of slavery and the oppression experienced following emancipation.

There are many different expressions of New Orleans Voudou, depending on the personal experience of the individual practicing it. Voudou is fluid, flexible, and adaptable. While most folks cannot fathom New Orleans Voudou without Marie Laveau and elements of Catholicism, it is not a given that all practitioners subscribe to these inclusions. Some practitioners of New Orleans Voudou do not include Marie Laveau in their pantheon of spirits. Some do not like that she made Hoodoo a business commodity and tourist attraction and oppose the inclusion of Catholic elements in the rituals. Perhaps they also practice another religion, such as Protestantism, Paganism, or Wicca. Many New Orleans Voudouists are initiated into a closely related African-derived sister religion such as Ifá or Santeria. Most are raised Catholic.

Voudouists who are Catholic and serve Marie Laveau practice what I call Laveau Voudou. Sometimes they are referred to as Catholic Voudous. They accept that Marie Laveau made a business out of Voudou and Hoodoo and are grateful that she did. Other than that, the fundamental beliefs, philosophies, and practices are identical among those who practice Voudou in New Orleans. In this book, when I refer to New Orleans Voudou, I am referring to the form that contains Catholic elements and views Marie Laveau as the Mother of New Orleans Voudou. Sometimes, I use the terms New Orleans Voudou and Laveau Voudou synonymously.

◇◇◇◇◇◇◇◇◇

It may seem weird to publish *The Marie Laveau Voodoo Grimoire* when Marie Laveau was reportedly illiterate. She did not write things down herself because she couldn't. So this grimoire becomes an imagining of what she would have written down had she been able to. I link her practices to documented sources throughout the book to show we are not too many degrees of separation away from her in terms of her magick and remedies. I introduce authentic Creole formulas, herbal remedies, and recipes commonly used during her lifetime. Through oral tradition, the Hoodoo, food, and domestic activities come directly from her point in history. And the conjures contained herein cover the issues for which people were known to have sought her advice—issues that remain relevant even today.

One thing I do not do is claim that I discovered a long-lost Laveau manuscript that has been hidden in someone's closet for 142 years and suggest that this book is a result of that fabricated discovery. I am fully transparent in that regard. My sources include oral tradition, corroborated by witness interviews conducted between 1936 and 1941 by the Federal Writers' Project (FWP), including Catherine Dillon's unpublished Voodoo manuscript.[8] I also reference Zora Neale Hurston's research; nineteenth-century newspaper reports of a legal nature, such as court appearances and raids; and everyday news articles from the 1800s that reflect the social and political climate of the time. Lastly, I pull from my own personal grimoires, where I have recorded formulas and recipes for the past forty years.

Much of the source material requires interpretation, as it was written by nonbelievers who ridiculed Voudou. It should also be noted that the newspaper accounts and Dillon's unpublished Voodoo manuscript are full of assumptions and racist tropes. From my observation, there is a dearth of sincere racist-free historical accountings of Voudou outside of the Federal Writers' Project interviewees. Still, some criticize this source, stating the FWP interviewees were not old enough to bear witness to Laveau herself. In fact, that is not the case. Anyone over sixty at the time the interviews took place could have known her. Most speak about being children when they saw or interacted with her. Others recount stories told by their parents or grandparents who knew her. Whether or not they were old enough to have witnessed Marie Laveau firsthand, they are the closest in terms of oral history to pass on what they knew or heard, making them among the most reliable sources.

All of the above notwithstanding, using any of these sources for a Marie Laveau grimoire requires the eye of a scholar-practitioner to make it make sense. Most of the rites found in original sources highlight only the ingredients, purpose, or procedures—and rarely all three. This is where my expertise comes into play. There is a continuity of Conjure works easily recognizable from the 1800s that persist in today's Hoodoo, Voudou, and Conjure traditions.[9] I know how to create the formulas and do the workings, and I've filled in those blanks when needed in this grimoire so that the reader can replicate them if they so desire.

In addition to a strong background in New Orleans Voudou, Hoodoo, and Spiritualism, my Catholic Creole culture of origin helped immensely when writing this book. Marie Laveau was a Louisiana Creole and Catholic also, and her spiritual practices reflect that. To be Creole in New Orleans means our blood derives from Spanish, French, Indigenous, and African ancestry, or some admixture within, and with that comes the traditions of our ancestors. From the rich mélange of food, music, culture, and religions, we find healing modalities and magickal works designed for empowered, resilient, and resourceful living.

In order to decide what specific content to include in *The Marie Laveau Voodoo Grimoire*, I turned to an obvious source: the product listings in Hoodoo drugstores in New Orleans at the turn of the twentieth century. Hoodoo drugstores, also referred to as Voudou drugstores back in their day, found a comfortable home in New Orleans in the late nineteenth and early twentieth centuries. Powders, oils, and potions of all kinds were sold in the pharmacies, and Hoodoo drugstores became a popular way to purchase such items. Some pharmacists developed a numbering system for their products so customers could order Voudou and Hoodoo products using a number instead of a name. This ensured a level of discretion with their transactions. For example, the New Orleans Pharmacy Museum displays Separation Powder as #45, Peace Powder as #7, and Come to Me as #62. According to the museum, this numbering system inspired the hit song "Love Potion No. 9." Despite built-in clandestine numbering systems, however, it was risky to be in the business of Hoodoo at the time because it was illegal and frowned upon as superstitious and fraudulent.

Since this book is a book of magick, it is presented as a grimoire. A grimoire is a book of magick that contains specialized occult knowledge, invocations, and instructions for working spells and rituals. Grimoires have been used by various practitioners of magick throughout history, from ancient Mesopotamia to medieval Europe to modern-day witches, hoodoos, and occultists. Grimoires are often considered powerful and dangerous objects, as they can grant access to hidden realms and entities or unleash curses and misfortunes upon those who misuse them. This grimoire is designed to only unleash blessings and magickal mysteries, to provide instructions for protection and defense, and to unlock joy and abundance for anyone reading it. There is no danger here.

More than just a collection of spells, however, *The Marie Laveau Voodoo Grimoire* contains tips and advice for living a magickal, spiritual lifestyle. It is ideal for anyone interested in cultural and spiritual well-being. Initiation is not required. Similar to the grimoire, the information in this book is likewise presented in the old-fashioned format of the domestic receipt book. Domestic receipt books described the herbs, simples, charms, and cures used in nineteenth-century households and contained practical advice and formulas for everything from cleaning furniture to brightening skin.

Inspired by the domestic receipt books of old, I sought to create something similar here but with a magickal twist. To that end, the following are the goals of this work: first, to provide instructions for conjuring a smooth, magickal household and living an abundant, spiritual life; second, to furnish an original collection of Creole spells, roots, remedies, cures, formulas, and receipts that celebrate our ancestors and ancestry; and third, to include only such receipts reproducible by today's practitioners.

I have purposefully avoided outdated, quaint recipes that may be interesting or quirky but are nonetheless useless for the modern practitioner. I also deliberately omitted recipes and formulas that require an overabundance of ingredients that are impossible to find or too expensive to procure.

In short, *The Marie Laveau Voodoo Grimoire* combines a practical domestic receipt book and a magickal grimoire in one concise, functional tome. The information is candidly presented, and the instructions for everything from making candle wicks to summoning spirits are easily understood. It is meant to be the ultimate reference book for living a life guided by intention, rich in purpose, and steeped in magick. My only regret is that it could not be longer.

May we all live long and fruitful lives despite pandemics, social injustices, and personal challenges. May we rise above that which seeks to oppress and silence us to find the joy in fiercely protecting and lovingly nurturing a happy, magickal home just like our Voudou Queen, Madame Marie Laveau.

Denise Alvarado
January 2023, during the season of Aquarius,
at the start of the lunar new year

The
MARIE LAVEAU
VOODOO
GRIMOIRE

Figure 1. African American woman and child outdoors, standing by boiling kettle of water, c. 1901.

Chapter 1

MATERIA MAGICA

Marie Laveau used all kinds of charms in her Hoodoo—candles and pictures and holy water just like in the Catholic Church.

—Joe Landry, 1939

I f you were a healer searching for herbs, red brick dust, and other materia magica of the healing arts in New Orleans in the 1800s, you would likely find yourself frequenting the busy rush of the old French Market. A strange, novel, cosmopolitan place, it was unlike anything else on the American continent. The odor of wild herbs and woodland leaves permeated the air. Choctaw women, the original inhabitants of the land upon which New Orleans now stands, sat cross-legged on the ground with their babies swaddled in cradleboards. Next to them were baskets woven from river cane in diamond patterns signifying a traditional reverence for the diamondback rattlesnake. Peering into these ancestrally coded baskets, one could see herbs used for cooking, medicine, and magick. From these women, bundles of bay laurel and manglier could be purchased to concoct aromatic teas for the infirm, as could sassafras leaves, which, when pounded with a mortar and pestle, was transformed into gumbo filé, used by the Creoles to make the now famous New Orleans dish, gumbo.

If you are a conjure worker or witch seeking magickal supplies today, you will find yourself bombarded with all sorts of covetable occult paraphernalia online. That said, I have yet to meet a conjure worker or witch who regrets having to procure all the herbs, curios, and pretties necessary for their spellcraft. All of these things create the ambiance, atmosphere, and energies

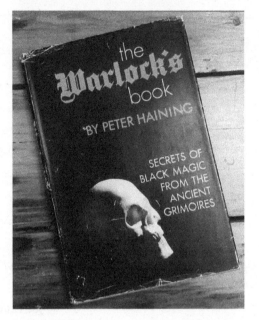

Figure 2. The author's first book on grimoire magick,
purchased when she was eleven, in 1971.

we love and crave. But, of course, there is more to magick than fancy ritual accoutrements. A thorough study and knowledge of the sympathetic characteristics of magick and ritual are required. As part of our traditional knowledge base, we must be familiar with the Doctrine of Signatures and herbs' magickal and medicinal attributes and their substitutions. The indigenous elements and tools used in rituals are part of the tradition, and effective practitioners will have full command of the sympathies of their paraphernalia. In the Laveau Voudou tradition, workers will have candles, dolls, jars, healing herbs, and more within reach. If you are working within a strict budget, the only tools you really need are yourself, a white candle, a glass of water, and the ability to focus your intention and utter words of power.

In this chapter, I share the essential tools of the trade to be an effective conjure worker in the Laveau Voudou tradition. These are suggestions based on more than fifty years as a practitioner, but please do not feel pressured to do everything I recommend. The important thing is that everything you do in a magickal sense should resonate with you. All the items you collect and tools you invest in should bring you joy, demonstrate respect for the ancestors, and pay homage to our Voudou Queen.

BELLS AND RATTLES

Bells and rattles are the practitioner's tools for prompting energetic changes in a space. They are used to signify the beginning, end, or changes in a rite. They are also used for spiritual cleansings, calling down spirits, and waking up sleepy or reluctant spirits.

Sound is mechanical energy. It causes a chain reaction throughout space that cannot be seen, but we know it happens because we can hear and feel it. When a bell or rattle rings, the vibrations from the sound cause movement in the surrounding air particles. These molecules bump into other molecules, causing them to vibrate as well. When the sound dissipates, the air molecules settle into new patterns; in that way, we can reprogram the energy in a room. The vibrations from the ringing of a bell or rattle break up stagnant, lingering energies, making sound a perfect vehicle for spiritually cleansing a space. Sound waves can travel through solids, liquids, and gases as vibrating particles, reaching spaces in ways other types of cleansings do not.

Bells and rattles can also be employed to signify changes in a rite. For example, during Catholic Mass, the ringing of a small bell during the consecration of the Eucharist signals the precise moment when bread turns into the body of Christ and wine turns into the blood of Christ. In Laveau Voudou, bells are also used to signify the beginning, change, or conclusion of a rite. The practitioner stands facing the altar or tree and makes the sign of the cross in the air three times while simultaneously ringing the bell. The sign of the cross in Voudou is a ritual code for the crossroads, where everything begins and ends. It is the place where the spirit world and the earthly world intersect. Ringing a bell helps set the stage for liminal work, aids in meditation, calls forth spirits, and gets the mind focused on ritual activity.

The asson is a sacred rattle used in Haitian Vodou to communicate with the spirits. This is not the kind of rattle the individual practitioner uses. It is a rattle made from glass beads or rattlesnake vertebrae with a bell attached at the handle and is used only by the priesthood.

BOOKS

Even before I was an author, I loved books. I grew up in a home that valued education, and my folks supported my eclectic interests. They bought me all sorts of occult books when I was growing up, from those little Dover pocketbooks to Anton LaVey's *Satanic Bible.* I still have the first book on grimoire magick I purchased from Mary Oneida Toups' witchcraft shop in the French

Quarter—*The Warlock's Book* by Peter Haining. The book inspired my love of woodcuts, and I was moved to learn how to make them myself as a teenager. The archaic, poetic language of the rituals fueled my already burgeoning wonderment of magick. I have always found books to have the power to bewitch and enchant—a good book will continue to give for as long as you possess it, and for as long as you open the pages with an open mind, ready to receive what it has to offer.

Witches and conjure workers have historically kept written accounts of their workings in their Books of Shadows and personal grimoires. Next to oral tradition, it is the primary way to preserve and pass down a magickal practice. Over the years, I have witnessed a lot of downplaying on the internet for people seeking knowledge about Voudou and Hoodoo via books, which makes no sense whatsoever. While I agree there is no replacing in-person learning from a teacher, only some have access to such experiences. And while you can't be initiated into anything via a book, books are the next best thing to personal experience for gaining access to knowledge of the occult mysteries. I bear no shame as a lover of books, and neither should you.

BOOK OF SHADOWS

I highly recommend keeping a Book of Shadows to record your experiences, rituals, and formulas. I cannot tell you how often I neglected to write down a recipe only to need it later. Especially now that I'm getting . . . wiser. Plus, it is good to record details of rituals so you can observe how effective certain things are and whether they are worth replicating in the future. For example, you may perform a love spell on a Friday during the full moon. Then you perform the same love spell without accounting for the day or moon phase. How do the outcomes compare? Hoodoo is not as concerned with moon phases as Witchcraft; things are typically done when needed. Nonetheless, it is entirely up to the worker how much ritual detail you want to incorporate into a working. Do what you need to do to bring out your best conjuring, and document it so that you can replicate it at a later date if necessary.

THE HOLY BIBLE

All hold the Bible as the great conjure book in the world. Moses is honored as the greatest conjurer. The names he knowed to call God by was what give him the power to conquer the Pharoah and divide the Red Sea.

—Zora Neale Hurston

One book is considered essential to most rootworkers: the Bible. Hold on, my Pagan, non-Catholic, non-Christian readers—it's not what you think. Conjure workers are not Bible-thumping preachers shouting from a soapbox on a street corner. At least most of us aren't, though some practitioners profess Hoodoo is not Hoodoo without the Bible, which sounds no different than modern-day evangelical Christians, to be honest. While many practitioners are indeed Christians, the Bible is used as a sacred talisman. Verses from the Bible are invocations, psalms are sacred incantations, and pages torn from the Bible are used in spells. In addition, bibliomancy using the Bible is a common form of divination.

In fact, holy books of many faiths have been incorporated into magick for centuries. The marabout of Islam uses passages from the Koran combined with magick seals and sigils to create their amulets, talismans, and gris gris (pronounced *gree-gree)*. The technique involves miniature handwritten texts that can be made into block prints for easy replication and then stamped onto high-quality parchment or perfumed paper. These miniature texts are then prayed over, with the marabout reciting specific verses sometimes hundreds of times over a single amulet. Then they are rolled and placed into special amulet boxes.

The Bible should be kept on your altar and used as a handy reference to passages needed for conjure work. There are different versions of the Bible—I prefer the King James version because I am used to it, and I like the retention of the archaic language. You can bookmark popular passages for easy reference later. Bibles can be purchased directly from a publisher or bookstore, or, if you are on a budget, you can find them in thrift stores. They come in assorted colors, too, so you can get a green one and fix it as your money Bible and get a red one and fix it as your love Bible, marking each with relevant passages for quick reference.

It is said that those who keep a pocket-size Bible in their top right pocket will receive blessings and protection from God. Once you have a Bible, you will need to know which psalms and passages are associated with which workings. Refer to my book *Voodoo Hoodoo Spellbook* for a complete list of psalms and their uses in Hoodoo, Voudou, Conjure, and Rootwork.

Applying the psalms and specific scriptural passages to personal problems is common in Hoodoo, Voudou, Conjure, and Rootwork. Practitioners employ the psalms by speaking or writing them as part of a working and then placing them in mojo or gris gris bags. Or they might burn them along with a petition in front of the image of a saint, then use the ashes to fix a candle or prepare a *gard* (a working of protection in Voudou) or *amparo* (a work of protection in the Latin American folk magic tradition). Workers may also instruct clients to recite specific psalms toward a given goal at certain times of the day. Psalm 23 is the most commonly prescribed, though others are equally popular. For example, to improve one's business success, Psalm 8 is used. Psalm 91 is said for protection and exorcisms. There is a magickal purpose for each psalm in Hoodoo, and the early publishers of occult literature seized the opportunity to introduce Jewish magick books to the African American folk magic community, where they were embraced.

Another reason to have a Bible on hand is for divination purposes. Bibliomancy is a popular form of divination amongst rootworkers. It entails focusing on a presenting issue, opening the Bible randomly with one's eyes closed, then taking the forefinger and pointing somewhere on the page. The diviner then reads the scripture on the page and applies it to the presenting problem or condition. If the page you open contains the words, "and it shall come to pass," your wish will be granted.

CANDLES

Candles are essential to have on hand. Candles are burned for prayerful intentions; the flame holds the intention and symbolizes the prayer. Between burning candles to the saints and setting lights for clients, Marie Laveau would have always had candles readily available. In fact, one of her neighbors recalled seeing so many candles burning in her home that she was surprised the house never burned down! Now, Marie wouldn't have had the variety of candles we have today, of course. Figural candles, knob candles, and glass-encased candles are the fruits of commercial Hoodoo and the Catholic Church. I like to keep things simple and recommend keeping a pack or two of regular white household candles on hand, as well as tea lights, chimes, and votives. These styles are great for short-term workings, such as when you need that candle to burn in less than a day.

CAULDRON

One item found consistently in the historical references to Marie Laveau's ritual activities is the cauldron. Aside from being a common cooking utensil, cast iron pots are still used to burn loose incense on charcoal discs, make black salt for banishing and protection rituals, mix herbs, or burn petitions. Marie Laveau had several cauldrons, including one where she placed her gris gris and another where she cooked her gumbo. Cauldrons are pricey but will last forever if you take care of them, and you can pass them down as heirlooms if you wish, which is nice.

CHARCOAL BRAZIER

A brazier is a portable metal or clay container that holds charcoal or wood fires. In the olden days, braziers came in all sizes and were used for cooking or heating the home. Marie Laveau's use of charcoal braziers is reported by an informant from Algiers, Louisiana, in Harry Middleton Hyatt's *Hoodoo-Conjuration-Witchcraft-Rootwork* Vol 1. In that publication, the informant refers to "furnace and fire" and "hot pots."[10] In magickal applications, braziers are ideal for burning charcoal for incense and resins. They are also suitable for burning dried herbs, flowers, and botanicals. Contemporary-style braziers include iron cauldrons, chimineas, and metal pots.

DOLL BABIES

Doll babies made from a variety of materials were frequently employed by Marie Laveau. She combined doll babies with containers like jars and coffins so often that container spells and coffin spells are separate categories of her Hoodoo. Doll baby spells attributed to Marie Laveau most frequently utilized black dolls. Keep a few premade poppet-style doll babies on hand for when image magick is called for. Just leave an opening in the dolls to place special talismans, petition papers, and herbs as needed.

INCENSE

Burning incense is one of the sacred rites of Laveau Voudou. It is also a ritual of the Roman Catholic Church. Thus, incense is something that any practitioner of New Orleans Voudou will have on hand for daily ritual use. Marie Laveau may have had access to church incense from her religious activities with Père

Antoine, St. Louis Cathedral, and her prison ministry. She would also have used simple three-ingredient or single-ingredient mixtures for various purposes. For example, burning onion and garlic peels with sulfur was common for exorcising meddlesome spirits and evil entities. Burning camphor was effective for cleansings, both spiritually and medicinally as an agent against diseases. Burning balm of Gilead buds was helpful for soothing heartbreak.

The use of incense associated with New Orleans Voudou can be found in a police report from the nineteenth century. In the middle of the hall, says the report, "was a vase, of which the contents were at least as varied as those of the caldron of Macbeth, a mixture in part composed of nameless substances. Around the vase, on three dishes of silver, many snakes carelessly reared their heads. The whole was surrounded by many hundred candles, and in the four quarters of the hall burned on hearths stimulating perfumes."[11]

I recommend having a few single-ingredient incense resins on hand, including dragon's blood, sandalwood, camphor, pine resin, amber, frankincense, and myrrh. Dragon's blood is for power, strength, and protection and can be combined with camphor to bless the home. Sandalwood is a highly fragrant bark perfect for blessing, cleansing, and consecrating people, places, and things. Camphor is a potent purifier, both magickally and medicinally. It expels evil entities and energies, cleanses, and purifies the air of dis-ease. Pine resin is a fantastic air purifier and is excellent for when you are sick with a cold. Amber just smells so damn good you gotta have some around. It elevates the mood and makes you want to have sex and dance. And, of course, frankincense and myrrh are classic biblical incenses used for blessing, purification, and consecration.

In addition to resins, I keep three Native American herbs around for smudging: sage, cedar, and sweetgrass. With these three plants, you have a great variety of naturally "stimulating perfumes," and you can custom blend them for your own special purposes. Sage and cedar are used for blessing, purification, protection, and curing, while sweetgrass is used for sweetening a space and inviting good spirits to come forth and visit.

KITCHEN HERBS AND SPICES

Many of the most commonly used herbs and spices in Marie Laveau's day would have had a dual use for cooking. For this reason, I encourage a nicely stocked kitchen cabinet. In old New Orleans, herb gardens were a common sight. The New Orleans Pharmacy, for example, had its medicinal herb gardens in the courtyard. When a particular herb was needed for a formula, it would be procured from the garden and compounded into a Hoodoo formula. As for all the witches, blitches, herbalists, and rootworkers reading this with your own magickal medicinal gardens, you already know how valuable it is to have a fresh supply of herbs on hand for oh so many purposes.

The following table includes herbs, spices, and everyday household items you should have on hand to create your own kitchen witch apothecary. A well-stocked cabinet will prepare you for anything and anyone coming your way.

Table 1. Kitchen witch essentials.

Materia Magica	Uses
Ammonia	Cleansing, cutting and clearing, removing blockages
Basil	Attracting money and prosperity
Black mustard seeds	Causing confusion in enemies, strife, or discord
Black pepper	Protecting from harm; crossing others
Brown paper bags	Drying herbs, writing petitions
Castor oil	Creating potions and magic lamps
Cayenne pepper (aka red pepper)	Heating up a situation, driving a person or condition away
Cinnamon	Spicing things up in a relationship; bringing something to you quickly; attracting money and good luck in gambling
Distilled water	Making spiritual waters and essences
Epsom salts	Making spiritual baths
Grapeseed oil	Excellent as a base oil for conjure formulas
Honey	Drawing love, money, and good things to you
Lemons	Cleansing, clearing negative energy
Mineral oil	Making certain mineral-based and left-handed Conjure oil formulas, such as Lodestone Oil and Black Arts Oil
Olive oil	Making holy anointing oils

Materia Magica	Uses
Rosemary	A women's herb for empowering, protecting, and bringing good luck
Salt	Cleansing, warding, protecting, removing, crossing, uncrossing (intention is everything here)
Sugar	Drawing things to you, abundance, love, prosperity
Vinegar	Souring situations; crossing
White household candles	Workings of any kind requiring a candle
White mustard seeds	Inspiring faith or hope

MINIATURE COFFINS

Miniature coffins have long been reported in association with Voudou in New Orleans. Consider the circumstances around the mysterious disappearance of a judge in 1875, for example. Judge McArthur, a magistrate for the First Municipal Court, went missing, and subsequent investigations revealed a few interesting details. He had been living with a Black woman in "concubinage" for some time. Her name was Louisa Williams. Although they reportedly got along well, Louisa became jealous of the judge and began working conjure on him. Little black coffins and other Voudou charms began to be found in his pillows and on his windowsills. At first, he thought little of it; but as they repeatedly appeared, he came to believe he was being fixed. He became moody and despondent. His health became poorer, and his mind was unsettled to a noticeable degree. Then, he disappeared from the public eye.

At first, he was believed to have come to an untimely end. But there was never an unidentified corpse discovered in the basin, river, or swamps since his mysterious disappearance. A newspaper reporter interviewed Louisa, who stated he was alive and well and staying not far from her. She denied administering any "vegetable drugs" on him when the topic of Voudou was brought up.[12] She said she did not know why he was staying out of sight, but she had seen him since his disappearance, and he looked well. Her testimony was enough to cast doubt on any thoughts of his death even though he never seemed to resurface.

Keep a few extra little coffins on hand for when you need one. They are pretty easy to find, especially around Halloween, when craft stores typically have cardboard and wood ones in stock. They are ideal for storing graveyard dirt and working conjures with doll babies, gris gris, and candles. While they are famously associated with left-handed magick, consider their use metaphorically, as opposed to harming someone. You can bury all sorts of things, like past relationships, secrets, and regrets. I have written elsewhere about using coffins in conjure, so I encourage you to check out my books *The Voodoo Doll Spellbook* and *The Magic of Marie Laveau* for more information.

OIL LAMPS

Marie Laveau and her daughter Marie Philomene used oil lamps, as they were a common household item and perfect for workings that require a slow accumulation of power over a prescribed number of days. Hurricane lamps are part of every New Orleans household, so grab a lamp or two and keep some lamp oil and wicks on hand so you can work one when needed. If you do not have access to hurricane lamps, tin cans are an old, inexpensive trick for making a lamp. In fact, oil lamps can be made from containers of all sorts, including shells and hollowed-out pumpkins, depending on the purpose.

PERFUMES, COLOGNES, AND SPIRITUAL WATERS

In Voudou, we use perfumes, colognes, and spiritual waters in service of the spirits instead of simply wearing them for vanity's sake. Thus, they are high on the list of essential ritual items to have on hand. They are used as offerings, to sanctify spaces, and to elevate energy for rituals. We add them to cleansing baths and floor washes, and clean and anoint ritual tools with them.

Perfumes, colognes, and spiritual waters are worn to raise specific vibrations (see table 2). For example, it is customary to splash on a little Hoyt's Cologne before gambling to bring good luck. Perfumes and colognes can also be used as hand rubs. Pour a few drops on your hands and rub briskly before engaging in a particular activity you wish to influence in a specific way. Hoodoo has hundreds of formulas for perfumes, colognes, and oils you can make for every condition under the sun. Most of these come from the commercial Hoodoo sector.

Sometimes colognes and perfumes are magically enhanced by adding herbs or using water from sources with specific magical properties. For a love-drawing perfume, for example, you could add a little filtered river water to supercharge it as rivers are associated with Oshun, the orisha of love. When adding herbs to perfume or cologne, the alcohol draws the aromatics from the plants and supercharges the fragrance toward the desired end. Two popular additions to colognes are tobacco and High John the Conqueror root. Added to any perfume, tobacco elevates, blesses, and empowers the scent above and beyond its original formulation. High John root supercharges the good luck and fortune factor of a perfume, cologne, or water. One reason for such increased enhancement with the addition of herbs and roots is that store-bought perfumes are not created according to the art of conjure. They are factory-made, using fragrance oils instead of essential oils, and do not have any botanical material in the bottles. They need to be energized in some fashion by the practitioner to activate them magickally.

Table 2. Perfumes and colognes and their magical uses.

Perfume or Cologne	Uses
Bien-Etre Lavande Sauvage	Added to spiritual baths or worn as perfume for good luck, money, love, protection, and to attract what you desire. Offered to La Sirene, Mami Wata, and Erzulie Dantor.
Bien-Etre Rose	Added to spiritual baths or simply worn as perfume for love, good luck, wealth, luxury, and to attract what you desire. Offered to Erzulie Freda.
Eau de Cologne	An all-purpose cologne used for mediumship, blessing, and cleansing.
Florida Water	An all-purpose, lovely cologne that is added to spiritual baths or worn as perfume for purification, blessing, and cleansing.
Hoyt's Cologne	Widely reputed to bring good luck to gamblers; also used to dress mojo bags.
Jockey Club	A cologne used for good luck, success in money matters, and winning in games of chance.
Kananga Water	Commonly found in Latin American folk magic, a cologne used for spiritual rituals, purification, and memorials to the dead. Used to dispel dark energy from a room, purify one's spirit and spatial energy, and facilitate ancestral communication. It can also be used for protection, prosperity, and increased sexuality.

Perfume or Cologne	Uses
Lotion Pompeii	A perfume used in Haitian Vodou and New Orleans Voudou to please the Rada spirits, especially Erzulie Freda. May be offered to Oshun.
Orange Blossom Cologne	A cologne used for spiritual services and to attract luck in love, money, business success, and marital peace.
Peace Water	Associated with Marie Laveau, this is given to her as an offering; sprinkled in the home it restores and maintains peace and harmony and removes negative energies.
Reve D'Or	A perfume used in Haitian Vodou and New Orleans Voudou to please the Petro and Kongo spirits, especially Erzulie Dantor.
Rose Water	Worn on the body, added to bathwater and floor washes; used as a floor sprinkle for luck and love; used to invoke love, respect, gratitude, sympathy, friendship, desire, and joy.
San Cypriano Spiritual Water	A spiritual water used to combat black magic and the devil and to remove all evil and negative energy from your life and home.
San Martin Caballero Perfume	A perfume to help you find a job and improve the cash flow in your business. Used to break hexes.
Seven African Powers Perfume	An all-purpose perfume with seven different powers: love, money, luck, health, protection, power, and success.
Siete Machos Cologne	A cologne with wide application, it is used for spiritual and emotional guidance and to block and reverse negative energy, hexes, and the evil eye. It can also be used to attract love, abundance, prosperity, good luck, and strength.
St. Michael the Archangel Spiritual Water	A spiritual water to fight evil and defend you in battles against evil. Used to defeat black magic and break curses.
St. Raymond Spiritual Water	Added to bathwater for expectant mothers for safe delivery; stops gossip that is affecting your life.
Willow Water	A medicinal water used to wash the head of those with headaches, for bathing aches and pains, and as an altar offering during invocations to the lunar and water goddesses.

PETITION PAPER

One of the most common ways of deploying a spell is by writing down your intention in a precise manner on a piece of paper. This is called a petition. Symbols, sigils, and talismans can also be drawn on paper as part of a petition or as the petition itself. The words and symbols may be written or drawn multiple times and in specific patterns to further signify the intention of the work. Marie Laveau reportedly drew talismans on parchment paper that she sewed into gris gris bags, placed under candles, or burned in a brazier or cauldron in spellwork.

The most common type of petition paper used in the magickal arts is parchment. However, parchment paper is costly, so if you can't afford it, any kind of paper will do. Using regular brown paper is an old-time Hoodoo practice. Ask for paper bags next time you go to the grocery store, then spend the evening cutting or tearing strips for use as petitions in a pinch.

Hoodoo also employs color correspondence according to race with petition papers. Brown paper for Brown and Black folks, and white for everyone else. This type of color coding is referred to by informants in the early twentieth century and is an expression of the law of similarity in sympathetic magick wherein "like begets like."

WORDS, THOUGHTS, AND INTENTIONS

Magick traditions have long emphasized the power of our thoughts, words, and intentions on our spellcraft and healing modalities. Dr. Masaru Emoto studied this phenomenon from a scientific standpoint and discovered thoughts and intentions do indeed impact the physical realm. His research consisted of exposing glasses of water to various words, pictures, or music, then freezing it and examining the ice crystals' visual properties with microscopic photography.[13] The words, phrases, and intentions seemed to affect the water when spoken into and over it.[14] Words written and placed under a bowl of water can have a similar effect, punctuating the importance of concisely written petitions. This is why we should avoid gossiping and frivolous speech when performing water rites, whether during a baptism, spiritual bath, foot washing, sweat lodge, or anything else. This is also why prayers are so powerful during cleansing rites.

When you can see what happens when hateful words are spoken over water, it makes you reconsider how your magick leaves an imprint on the world. Focusing on revenge and cursing others leaves a lot of ugly we cannot see, yet we sure can feel. I'm not saying there is never a time to do left-handed magick; in the world of Hoodoo, it's all about restoring balance and returning conditions to their natural order. This is one reason you must be incredibly careful with the work you do and be justified in doing it. Our bodies are 60 percent water, so even when we direct our words into a candle or a doll, they come from and vibrate within our physical, water-laden vessels. Makes you think about what kind of weight you want to carry around, doesn't it? It should also empower you to realize that correct thought and speech can have a healing and restorative effect on our bodies.

Dr. Emoto's research has faced some criticism from the scientific community, but his ideas are similar to those found in magick. While modern magick is often dismissed as fraudulent by scientists, the study of ancient magick is taken seriously within academic circles. The challenge in accepting magick in a scientific context lies in defining and measuring its concepts. The fact that mainstream science has yet to fully explain magick doesn't negate its existence. It simply highlights the need for scientists to broaden their perspectives and approach the study of magick with greater creativity and flexibility.

Figure 3. Portrait of Betsy by François Fleischbein, 1837.
A young Creole woman in a tignon of her own creation.

Chapter 2

BEAUTY FORMULAS

Marie Laveau was a mulatto with fine features. She was certainly a good-looking woman, that is she must have been pretty. You could see it from her features. Even though she was growing old you could see that she took good care of herself.

—Mrs. Marie Dede, 1939

It's only fitting that *The Marie Laveau Voodoo Grimoire* would have a chapter on Creole beauty formulas. She was a well-known hairdresser and expert beautician, after all, and she catered to the bourgeoisie in the most exclusive boudoirs. With a smile on her face and a twinkle in her eye, she listened to the scurrilous trysts and scandals shared by the indulgent beauties that made up a large portion of her clientele. The women carried on recklessly with their incessant gossiping, but Marie didn't mind. Hair is a prominent social activity in African and southern culture, and that's what women do when fixing each other's hair. She took advantage of the women's loose-lipped nature, and soon she was collecting small sums of money as payment for her silence. Of course, it wouldn't work long-term for her to be a known blackmailer. So, she developed a network of informants who worked among the elite to bring her information about them. This way, she had all the background she needed to help those same women and their husbands, who, unbeknownst to each other, went to her for magickal solutions to their relationship problems. Marie had them all over a barrel six ways to Sunday. Soon it became clear who the real Boss Woman was.

According to legend, Marie Laveau owned a beauty parlor on Royal Street near St. Louis Cathedral. When she needed a lock of hair tied with a red ribbon to dominate a lover for a client, she had little problem getting it. As a beautician, she had the trust of her clients and could easily acquire such powerful items for her spellcraft. Access to personal effects in this manner is a form of unspoken power she yielded. Even today, people who serve Marie Laveau offer her beauty-related items such as combs, mirrors, makeup, brushes, and perfumes in hopes that she will grant them favors.

Harsh diseases that were commonplace during the 1800s left women's faces scarred by age and disease. These conditions led to a high demand for remedies. In this chapter, I share some heritage beauty remedies Creole women used during that period which were likely a part of Marie Laveau's beauty rescue arsenal. Additionally, I provide modern versions of these remedies that are practical for today's lifestyle.

DRY PERFUMES

Dry perfumes, or perfume dusting powders, are used as natural perfumes and deodorants. They reduce moisture on the body, which causes body odor and acne. Unlike spray perfume, much of which is wasted in the air around you, scented body powders are applied directly onto the skin. Use a luxurious powder puff to press the silky, fragrant powder directly onto your skin for odor control, moisture protection, and the long-lasting fragrance of essential oils. The aromas blend with your body's natural oils, enhancing the scent's staying power.

Lavender Dust
For this lovely scented body powder, you need the following ingredients:

    1 ounce orris root
    2 ounces lavender flowers
    Lavender essential oil
    1 ounce cornstarch

Render the orris root and lavender flowers to a fine powder with a mortar and pestle or herb grinder. Add lavender essential oil to your preferred strength. Combine with cornstarch and sift with a handheld sifter. Store in a glass jar. Use as an allover body powder.

Sweet Sandalwood Powder

This is a warm, sweet, earthy scented body powder. To make it, you need the following ingredients:

> 2 ounces orange peel
> 1 ounce orris root
> ½ ounce sandalwood
> ¼ ounce tonka beans
> Sandalwood essential oil
> 1 ounce cornstarch

Render the orange peel, orris root, sandalwood, and tonka beans to a powder with a mortar and pestle or herb grinder. Add a few drops of a good sandalwood essential oil and mix well. Combine with cornstarch and sift with a handheld sifter. Store in a glass jar. Use as an allover body powder.

HAIR TREATMENTS

Historically, hair has played a significant role in African cultures. It can signify one's family background, spirituality, tribe, and social and marital status. Because hair is so intimately tied to one's identity and spirituality, care is taken to allow only certain trusted individuals to touch it. Its power is evident. If just one strand were to fall into the hands of an enemy, a lot of damage could be done to the person to whom it belongs. To care for your own sacred crown, try some of the following hair treatments:

Banana Hair Mask for Dry Hair

Bananas contain beneficial properties that may help prevent split ends by softening hair and improving elasticity. They are high in potassium and have high moisture content, which makes them suitable for treating dry hair. Mash 1 banana well and thoroughly work it into the hair from roots to ends. Leave on for 1 hour and rinse with warm water. Yes, you will smell like a banana—but your hair will thank you for it.

Warm Oil Treatment for Dry Hair

Use warm oil treatments for dry, brittle, lackluster hair. Warm 6 tablespoons of olive oil in a pan on the stove. Alternately, you can use 3 tablespoons of olive oil and 3 tablespoons of castor oil. Coconut oil and almond oil are also good for hair.

Dip a cotton ball into the oil and rub it into the scalp. After you've saturated the hair, massage oil into the scalp with your fingertips. Next, dip a terry cloth towel in hot water, squeeze it out, and wrap it around the head. The heat opens the pores so that the oil can perform more than surface benefits. When the heat cools, reapply a second towel. Shampoo and rinse hair three times to get out all the oil.

Egg Wash for Brittle Hair

Eggs are rich in protein, which helps to fortify and strengthen hair and restore moisture to dry, brittle hair. Make an egg shampoo by beating the yolk of 1 or 2 eggs in warm water. Apply from roots to ends and leave on for 30 minutes. Rinse hair several times with warm then cold water. Dry the hair and brush for ½ hour.

Banana and Egg Rescue for Thinning Hair

Whip 2 egg yolks, 2 ripe bananas, 2 tablespoons honey, ½ cup conditioner, and 2 tablespoons olive oil until thoroughly blended. Slather all over your scalp and leave on for 30 minutes. Rinse with cool water. The results are said to be immediate but will only last until your next shampoo.

To Fix a Flaky Scalp

To keep flakes under control, try making this ginger root scalp spray. It uses the anti-inflammatory properties of ginger root to slow down cell turnover and fight dandruff.

All you have to do is make ginger root tea. Finely grate half a ginger root into 2 cups of water and reduce the liquid until it is 1 cup of tea. Add a tablespoon of lemon juice and olive oil and blend well. Spray the remedy directly onto the scalp, let dry, and shampoo out.

General Tips for Hair Health

In addition to topical treatments, hair health can be positively affected by changing diet and behavior. To prevent excessive drying, shampoo less frequently, use a humidifier to keep the scalp from drying out, avoid too much sun exposure, and trim hair often to keep split ends at bay. In addition, follow a healthy, balanced diet because, as the saying goes, "You are what you eat." Thus, drink plenty of water and include fatty fish, such as salmon, mackerel, sardines, and tuna, in your diet, as well as oysters, blueberries, tomatoes, walnuts, broccoli, and kidney beans.

Black hair is unique in structure and requires special consideration. Wash your hair at most once a week or every other week. Use a hot oil treatment once a month. Make sure cornrows, braids, and weaves are not too tight. Always use a conditioner after shampooing. Use a heat-protecting product on your hair while still wet before styling. Finally, use ceramic combs or irons to press the hair and only use once a week.[15]

SKIN CARE

Skin care was of primary importance for women in the 1800s as part of their personal hygiene and beauty routines. Women often made their own skin care products from natural ingredients such as glycerin, rose water, sulfur, and salt. These homemade remedies were used to soften, moisturize, cleanse, and brighten the skin. Try a few of these heritage formulas to get your skin glowing.

Calendula and Plantain Ointment for Dry Skin
This ointment is great for soothing dry, irritated skin.

> ½ cup dried calendula petals
> ½ cup dried plantain leaves
> Olive oil to cover
> Beeswax

Place calendula petals and plantain leaves in a glass bowl over simmering water or double boiler, and cover with oil. Warm the oil, stirring often, for 2 to 3 hours. Strain. Place the oil back in the bowl over steaming water and add enough beeswax to create the desired consistency. Pour into jars and use as needed for dry skin.

Cold Cream
Cold cream is a cosmetic preparation for cleansing and softening the skin. Cold cream formulas always contain a mixture of water and fats. When you put the cream on your skin, the water evaporates, which creates a cooling sensation, hence the name. To make a vintage cold cream, you will need the following:

½ pint finely pulverized sweet almonds
1 ounce white rose perfume
½ ounce Vaseline
½ pint rose water

Mix the almonds, white rose perfume, Vaseline, and rose water. Beat the mixture until it is thoroughly blended and fluffy. Apply to face before bedtime. You can also use this preparation as a makeup remover and cleanser.

Easy Rose Lotion
An easy-to-make lotion consists of 1 part glycerin and 9 parts rose water. Mix well and apply to the skin.

Face Wash
Vintage beauty recipes sometimes use unusual units of measurement and ingredients. For example, in this formula, a wine glass is used for measurement, and flowers of sulfur is an ingredient. Flowers of sulfur is a very fine, bright yellow sulfur powder used to treat skin conditions. Blend 1 teaspoon of powdered flowers of sulfur with half a wine glass of glycerin and a wine glass of rose water as a wash for the complexion. Apply liberally to the face every night before going to bed. Rinse well with warm water in the morning.

In Hoodoo, sulfur is burned to cleanse a home of evil and negativity. It is mixed with salt and sprinkled wherever a jinx has been laid to break the spell. It is also a common ingredient in Goofer Dust, Hot Foot powder, and Drive Away formulas.

Ointment for Rough Hands

1½ ounces beeswax
1 ounce camphor
¾ pint sweet almond oil

Cut up the beeswax and camphor, and place in a pan. Add the sweet almond oil. Heat on low until everything has melted. Blend well with a spoon. When it is well-blended and a smooth consistency, pour into small jars and allow to cool. Rub ointment into your hands to soften them. This ointment works well on feet, too.

Salt Glow

Salt rubs are a type of body scrub made from salt. They are designed to exfoliate, remove dead skin cells, and leave behind soft, invigorated skin. The Salt Glow is a healing rub and detoxifying technique that requires salt and warm water. The goal is to increase circulation of the blood, mucus membranes, and lymphatic system. Get in the shower or tub, and using a coarse salt of your choice, begin rubbing it all over your body, starting with your fingers. Mix the salt with warm water to help move it over your body. Move from your fingers to your hands, and with broad strokes in one direction, move up your arms toward your heart. Do the same thing with your toes, feet, ankles, and legs. Massage your whole body and end with your face. When done, be sure to rinse well with warm water. Your skin should have a slightly pink glow, showing dead skin has been removed, pores have opened up, and your blood is circulating.

To Remove Wrinkles

To reduce the appearance of wrinkles, mix 1 ounce of melted beeswax, 2 ounces of honey, ½ ounce of rose water, and a drop or 2 of attar of roses and blend well. Use twice daily.

Figure 4. The best time for conjuring is when the need arises. Burning a petition activates the intention.

Chapter 3

THE BEST TIMES FOR CONJURING

Marie Laveau held her services on Wednesdays and Fridays. Never on Sundays. But people went to see her all the time.

—Mrs. Marie Dede, 1939

People often wonder whether or not there are optimal times—days of the week, phases of the moon, and so forth—when it comes to conjuring. As a practitioner, you can cast a spell at a moment's notice, but there can be advantages to using certain timing correspondences to optimize power and impact. The association of special times with ritual activities is called *magickal timing*.

One of the primary things to consider about pairing ritual work with specific timing is intention. People are often driven by emotion and act on impulse; thus, they do not think the work through clearly. As a result, they experience any number of unwanted consequences; the most common is simply an ineffective conjure. We live in an instant gratification society and want what we want when we want it. We don't like to wait. However, waiting for the right time can sometimes be one of the most important things you can do to render an effective spell. The intricacies of magickal timing are why many folks hire a professional rootworker to perform a spiritual service instead of attempting the work themselves.

Magickal timing can be broken down into several categories, including days of the week, moon phases, sunrise and sunset, planetary hours, time of the year, major life events, hands of the clock, biblical associations, and even a woman's menstrual cycle. The most commonly considered magickal timing categories are days of the week, phases of the moon, and sunrise and sunset. Which method a worker subscribes to is entirely personal; it boils down to what works.

In Hoodoo, timing is associated with activities of daily living and the days these activities typically occur. For example, people generally get paid on Fridays, so Fridays are associated with prosperity work, getting a job, and getting a raise. In classical traditions, Friday is associated with Venus, the love goddess, and therefore is the ideal day to perform spells related to love a nd relationships.

While there are other ways to incorporate magickal timing into ritual work, the ones described in this chapter are easy to implement. Try pairing your ritual work with one of the described methods, and you should see an improvement in the power and success of your ritualistic endeavors.

DAYS OF THE WEEK

The days of the week are associated with magickal timing in many esoteric and occult traditions, but it was the Babylonians who first created the concept of a seven-day week. They named each day after one of the seven celestial bodies known at the time: the sun, the moon, Mars, Mercury, Venus, Jupiter, and Saturn. According to Babylonian beliefs, these heavenly bodies impacted people's lives on the corresponding day.[16]

Sunday
Sunday is the sun's day, and its power can amplify any ritual work. It is a good day for gaining wisdom and seeking assistance with health, wellness, blessings, prosperity, individuality, and power. In New Orleans Voudou and related African-derived religions, Sundays are devoted to God and the orishas Obatala and Orunmila and the loa Gran Bwa.

Monday
Monday is the moon's day, a great day for water rituals, healing, fertility, transformation, intuition, and family matters, particularly those concerning women and children. In New Orleans Voudou and related African-derived religions, Mondays are devoted to the gatekeeper spirits Papa Legba, Ellegua, Eshu, and Exú, the ancestors, and the barons.

Tuesday

Tuesday is ruled by Mars and is appropriate for works involving aggression, offensive battle strategies, enemy work, protection, justice, and manipulating testosterone. In New Orleans Voudou and related African-derived religions, Tuesdays are devoted to Ogun, Erzulie Dantor, and the spirits of the Petro nations.

Wednesday

Wednesday is Mercury's day, ideal for communication, teaching the arts, transformation, traveling, learning, and luck. In New Orleans Voudou and related African-derived religions, Wednesdays are devoted to Ogun, Annie Christmas, Oya, Damballah Wedo, and Babalú-Aye.

Thursday

Thursday is ruled by Jupiter, and is ideal for conjuring increased wealth, finding treasures, abundance, success, and seeking answers to burning questions. In Catholic Conjure and Laveau Voudou, yellow candles are offered to St. Roche and St. Expedite on Thursdays. In New Orleans Voudou and related African-derived religions, Thursdays are devoted to the spirits Damballah Wedo, Olodumare, Olofin, Oshun, Obatala, Agassou, and Orunmila.

Friday

Friday is Venus's day, and the classical love goddess makes Friday ideal for working on matters of the heart—love, desire, beauty, and romance. Friday is also the day many people get paid for their week's work, so it is a good day for prosperity work. In New Orleans Voudou and related African-derived religions, Fridays are devoted to Chango, Oya, Babalú Aye, the barons, Erzulie Freda, and Manman Brigitte.

Saturday

Saturday is Saturn's day, perfect for conjures related to righteous anger, justified revenge, causing sickness, creating obstacles, banishing, binding, and destroying enemies. In New Orleans Voudou and related African-derived religions, Saturdays are devoted to Yemaya, Oshun, and Baron Samedi, and it is the day to celebrate all spirits.

PHASES OF THE MOON

A moon's phase refers to the shape of the illuminated portion of the moon as seen from earth. Since the moon and earth are forever locked by the tides, we always see the same lunar surface. Four principal lunar phases hold significance to magickal workers: the first quarter (waxing), full moon, third quarter (waning), and new moon. There is also the period at the end of the waning phase, just before the new moon crescent, that holds significance to workers. This is referred to as the dark moon because the moon is not visible.

The new moon is when the moon officially begins to wax, growing in visibility until it reaches full moon status. The new moon is an excellent time to start new projects and prepare new conjures.

Waxing moons begin after the new moon and visibly grow until the full moon. Rituals designed to draw things to you are best done during this moon phase.

Waning moons begin after the full moon and end the day of the dark moon. Rituals designed to eliminate obstacles, conditions, or people are best worked during this moon phase.

The dark moon is the day before the new moon. Take advantage of the moon's invisibility to perform clandestine works such as crossings and reversals.

SUNRISE AND SUNSET

Working by sunrise or sunset is another way to enhance magickal work. Do works designed to draw things to you from dawn until noon, such as love, money, and success. Do works intended to remove or eliminate conditions such as debt or illness from noon until sunset.

HANDS OF THE CLOCK

When both hands of the clock point upward, it is the ideal time to perform work to draw something to you. When both hands face downward, it is the perfect time to repel negativity.

BEST TIMES FOR CLEANSING

The traditional time for taking a spiritual bath is at or right before dawn. Some folks pay attention to the moon phases for enhancing the power of their cleansing. For example, when the desired result is removing a condition or obstacles, then cleansing during a waning moon is ideal. A waxing moon is ideal if the goal is drawing something to you. A full moon is perfect for harnessing all the moon's power towards a desired goal. However, a cleansing can be done any time the need arises, so don't wait until morning comes if there is an urgent need.

Figure 5. Take care of your ritual items by storing them in boxes and jars to keep them free from dust and the elements.

Chapter 4

CARING FOR YOUR RITUAL ITEMS

*When I knew Marie Laveau, she was a good-looking woman, about
45 or 50. She was a neat dresser. She was always dressed in a long blue
or white dress. She had fine jewelry and wore it all the time. She made
plenty of money. She always wore large diamond earrings, a diamond
pin, and rings.*

—Mr. John Smith, age 72

W hat seems obvious is only sometimes the case—especially when
it comes to magick. For example, how often do you clean your
ritual tools? Are they dusty? Are they stored correctly? Do you
even know where everything is? You need to take care of your ritual items so
they can take care of you. They are your partners in magick, and when you
ignore and neglect them, you have no one to blame but yourself when your
magick is weak and ineffective. Ignoring and neglecting your tools is ignoring
and neglecting your power.

All ritual tools should be cleansed and blessed before use. Consider the
secondhand items you may have acquired as gifts, bought online, or purchased in thrift stores, for example. Suppose you don't cleanse the residual
energy from these items. In that case, you may unknowingly siphon someone
else's energy or be targeted for your own power.

Make your own tools if and when you can. Things you cannot make,
such as knives, cauldrons, incense censors, bells, and the like, can be easily
purchased from any number of online vendors. These tools will need to be
cleansed and blessed.

Just as your store-bought tools need cleansing and special care, so does the materia magica of the natural world you utilize. Bones, stones, herbs, and roots will benefit from cleaning and storing them correctly to preserve maximum strength and efficacy.

Cleansing includes mechanical and spiritual cleansing. Inspect ritual items regularly for tarnishing, dust, discoloration, brittleness, funky smells, and other signs of wear and tear. Wipe down glass-encased candles with Florida Water. Clean blades with olive oil. Keep your cast iron seasoned. Smudge tools with incense, herbs, or spiritual waters. Always combine prayer and mindful intention when cleansing.

THE ALTAR

In every room of the old house, Marie Laveau's daughter keeps an altar to the memory of her mother, with dozens of lighted candles burning continually for the repose of her soul.

—*The Times-Picayune (New Orleans), 1900*

Yes, your altar needs care. It is a living point of spiritual contact, a liminal, sacred space, and needs to be treated as such. Whether it is a simple incense altar or an elaborate All Saints altar, caring for this sacred space is a ritual act that reflects the inner state of your spiritual well-being.

The cleanliness of your altar reflects your attitude toward your spiritual well-being and your relationship with the spirits you serve. A dusty, cluttered altar with no rhyme or reason can have an impact on how things manifest or fail to manifest for you. Some spirits will ignore you if their altar space is filthy. Everything to do with your altar should be done in ceremony, from choosing what to put on it, to cleaning and setting it up, to the words you speak when standing in front of it.

Some practitioners believe that the more altars you have, the better witch or conjure worker you are. There was a point in my life when I was totally guilty of this. I had over twenty altars in my home! After a while, the spirits informed me that was not how any of this worked. In Voudou, we don't need a separate altar for each spirit. All you really need is one altar for your spiritual court and another for your ancestors.

For years now, I have maintained an All Saints altar. Marie Laveau and Mami Wata are at the head of this altar, as they represent the connection between New Orleans Voudou and African Vodun. I have a separate altar below my main altar for the guede, the sacred dead, and the barons, who are the spirits of death and preside over the guede. Another altar is for Maximón because he is an ancestor. Ancestor altars are separate from altars for the spirits. Finally, I have an incense altar and a Hoodoo altar where workings are done.

All altars need to be baptized before use. After setting up your altar or shrine, you can baptize it by praying three Our Fathers and seven Hail Marys, anointing the altar with extra virgin olive oil, and sprinkling it with holy water. You can also use Altar Oil, 7-11 Holy Oil, Holy Oil, or High Altar Oil to anoint your shrine.

Some simple, practical suggestions for keeping up with your altar are to start with cleaning away dirt and dust. Wipe everything down with water, Florida Water, Chinese Wash, or whatever your preferred spiritual cleanser may be. Use a soft, lint-free cloth. If you have cracks and crevices to clean, use a soft toothbrush. Don't forget to clean the entire altar, including underneath it, the legs, sides, floor, baseboards, wall, and any photos or images hanging on it. Wash your altar cloth regularly.

Throw away all food offerings after three days. Take them outside and place them under a bush or tree where the animals will help get rid of them.

Change out fresh flowers weekly. If you have some evergreens or long-lasting flowers, sort through the blossoms and leaves and remove any dead ones. Place these in a compost pile or an outside garden. Remember that flowers are offerings and shouldn't be allowed to wilt and wither while asking for something to manifest. Dead offerings pretty much defeat the purpose of manifestation.

Always keep a glass of water on your altar for the spirits and refresh it weekly. Don't let it evaporate completely, and ensure the glass holding the water is clean and clear. If you have an issue with high mineral content in your water, as I do, you will have a ring of salt and a film that forms on your glass. Add vinegar to the glass and allow it to sit for an hour or so. The mineral deposits will come right off when washing, and your glass will be sparkling clean.

Lastly, treat your body like the temple that it is. Don't approach your altar when you are covered in filth and dirt. Take the time to bathe first and approach your altar with reverence.

BONES, ANTLERS, AND HORNS

Hoodoo is full of workings that utilize bones and horns. Many people like to gather and prepare their bones instead of buying them from a vendor. Who among you has not found a bone and squealed a little at the discovery?

Sometimes found bones are yellowed and may have traces of skin, feathers, or flesh on them, depending on the stage of decomposition. Even if you prepare your bones from a chicken dinner, you may have trouble getting them the shade of white you prefer. Lucky for you, there are ways to clean and whiten them that preserve their structural integrity and improve their color. One way is through maceration. Maceration allows bacteria present in water to clean the bones. Frankly, it's a stanky process, and instead of using up space in this book on the topic, I am going to say google it.

There are a couple of things to remember about bones, however. To glue teeth or vertebrae into place, use white glue. If you want to whiten them, do not use bleach. Bleach degrades bones, and chlorine can turn them into powder. Soaking your bones in hydrogen peroxide is the preferred method for whitening bones. Soak for 15 minutes or so, then remove from the solution and dry with a soft towel. Allow them to air dry completely. *Do not store wet bones; allow them to fully air dry before storing.*

Store bones in a cool, dry place. Do not store bones in plastic wrap. They need to breathe! Do not leave them outside in the sun for prolonged periods if you want them to last, as they will get brittle and break.

Finally, bones are porous and absorb the oils from your skin, so always handle bones with clean, dry hands.

CAST IRON CAULDRONS

Cast iron pots, pans, and cauldrons require special care to work efficiently. They must be prepared through a process called "seasoning." Seasoning increases the life span of a pot by protecting it from rust and adding a coating that safeguards it from heat damage. It is simple to do and is the first thing you should do after acquiring one.

First, wash your cauldron with soap and water and dry it well. Then pour a little olive oil onto a cloth or paper towel. Rub the oil all over the cauldron, inside and out. You can use any cooking oil, but I prefer olive oil for preparing magickal tools. Be sure you have wiped off the excess oil. Treat the lid if you have one in the same fashion.

Then stick the pot into your oven at 350 degrees and cook for about an hour. Place the lid next to the cauldron instead of on top of it. After the hour is complete, remove it from the heat and allow it to cool off for an hour. Then take a little more oil and coat just the inside. It is now ready to use.

If using your cauldron to burn incense, shield the bottom by placing a 1- to 2-inch layer of sand or incense ash on the bottom before burning your incense and botanicals in the pot.

CEREMONIAL GARB AND CLOTHING

For centuries, magicians have worn special clothing for their ceremonial activities. Marie Laveau is said to have worn a long purple dress with a rope around her waist during her rituals along Lake Pontchartrain. She wore low shoes with no strings. Other women in her congregation wore purple dresses while the men wore white cotton or linen. Ceremonial garments made from cotton, satin, and velvet require special cleaning methods.

Some basic rules of washing clothes apply to ceremonial garb. Keep your colors and your whites separate. If you don't, the colors can bleed onto your whites and stain them. Restoring them to their previous brightness can be nearly impossible when that happens. So, avoid the problem altogether by washing your whites separately from colored clothing. You should always wash dark colors in cold water.

Wash satin clothing in cold water with a detergent for delicate clothing and wash on the delicate cycle. Avoid twisting and wringing satin, and carefully swish the fabric in the water instead. Satin can be handwashed.

Velvet is a soft, luxurious fabric that screams witchy glamour, and there are only two ways to clean it besides drycleaning: spot-cleaning and handwashing. The sooner a stain is treated, the easier it is to remove. To spot-treat a stain on velvet, blot away any excess residue using a cold, moist, lint-free cloth. Brush the fabric in one direction only to prevent the pile from being damaged further. If the stain is stubborn, use a tiny amount of detergent designed for delicate fabrics at the site of the stain. Use a damp cloth to absorb any excess soapy residue.

Vintage velvet garments require handwashing. Turn the garment inside out and place a sparse amount of gentle detergent on the flat, untextured side of the velvet. Press the soap gently through the fabric and rinse the garment thoroughly to remove all excess soap.

If you have a vintage silk or velvet garment with delicate beading, sequins, or intricate embroidery, take it to a dry cleaner if it needs cleaning. Otherwise, wash by hand in cold water with a detergent designed for delicate fabrics. Synthetic and cotton velvets without beading, sequins, or embroidery can likely withstand a washing machine's gentle cycle.

Wash cotton clothing in cold water to avoid shrinkage. Pretreat any stains, sort them into light, white, and dark colors, and wash them separately.

Always air dry anything you are unsure of to avoid shrinkage or heat-related damage. Otherwise, tumble dry on low or roll garments in a towel to press out excess water and lay flat to dry.

Use White Vinegar to Refresh Your Whites

"Whites" is the term Voudouists use to describe their white ceremonial clothing. To keep whites bright, add half a cup of white vinegar to your wash water. Vinegar helps remove gray and yellow stains and helps keep colors vibrant. As a bonus to physically cleaning your whites, vinegar also removes stagnant, negative energy and provides spiritual protection. Alternatively, you may use ½ cup of oxygen bleach or borax to serve the same purpose. Avoid using pure bleach with your whites. Instead, soak your whites in hot water with 2 cups of baking soda for a couple of hours if they are yellowing or graying. Afterward, place them in the washing machine with an enzyme-rich detergent that is effective on different stains without using hot water. Of course, the best way to get rid of the gray is to prevent your whites from discoloring in the first place. To do that, follow the tips I have provided.

To Remove Blood Stains

If you get blood on your clothes, immediately place the garment in cold water. Soak for 30 minutes before using a stain remover. Do not bleach a blood stain. Do not use stain removers that contain bleach. Bleach weakens fabric fibers, causing them to break and holes to appear.

CLEANSING AGENTS

While there are specific ways to cleanse particular items, there are also some general ways. Next, I share different ways to ritually cleanse your magickal tools so you have options when needed.

Ammonia

Throughout history, ammonia has proven to be a most versatile cleansing agent. From cleaning a household to working conjure, ammonia has merits on both the mundane and magickal levels. It is used in spells of protection, cleansing, bringing in business, and psychic clearing, among a host of other things. In New Orleans, many years ago, it was common for folks to wash their front steps with a solution of urine or ammonia, salt, bluestone or red brick dust, or other ingredients that possess magickal qualities. The combination of ingredients forms a protective barrier, spiritually marking that territory as a ward to thwart evil and negative energies.

As is often the case with folk practices, change occurs over time. Since people no longer use chambers to hold their urine, and there are bathrooms with running water, the use of urine as a practical ingredient has diminished. Not growing up in the same context as their grandparents, the younger generation began substituting ammonia for urine when performing magick works involving cleansings. Ammonia is a solution of anhydrous ammonia (NH_3) in water, and at least since the commercialization of Hoodoo in the 1930s became the standard replacement for urine in Hoodoo and Conjure. Marketers target various brands of ammonia to the folk magick demographic for their use in cleansing, clearing, protection, uncrossing, and removing jinxes.

In recent years, there has been a trend to mix ammonia with bleach for use in jar spells. Do not do this! Mixing ammonia with bleach results in toxic chloramine vapors that are harmful when inhaled. There is no historical precedence for this combination of chemicals, and I cannot justify it as a new practice.

In the past, old-timers often mixed ammonia with vinegar for souring purposes. Unlike bleach, vinegar does not produce a toxic vapor when combined with ammonia. Even so, it is counterproductive in practical terms. Vinegar is acidic, and ammonia is basic, which means they cancel each other out, essentially creating saltwater. This result effectively robs both ingredients of their souring properties.

So, how can we use ammonia for spiritual cleansing? One way is in a cleansing bath. Use one-half capful of ammonia in a full bath to cleanse negative energy off you. It's strong stuff, and you don't need much. Too much ammonia can ward off good spirits and good luck. Take an ammonia bath no more than once every three months unless expressly prescribed by a reputable rootdoctor.

One of my favorite conjure hacks for clearing negative energy from clothes and linens is adding one capful of ammonia to your weekly wash loads to keep your clothing and bedding free of blockages.

To clear clinging, stubborn, oppressive energies off your home's surfaces, pour a capful of ammonia into a bucket of hot water. Toss a bit of hyssop or rue into the water and swish everything around using a large crucifix. Take a clean white cloth and soak it in the water while praying Psalm 23. Remove the cloth and wring it out. It is now ready to wipe down counters, doors, refrigerators, other kitchen appliances, lamps, furniture, floors, walls, light switches, windows, and blinds. While wiping down the surfaces, you should be mindful of wiping away evil messes and stagnant energy.

If you don't have any Florida Water to cleanse your candles and don't want to use saltwater or holy water, take a white, lint-free dish towel, pour just enough ammonia to moisten the towel, and wipe down your candles with the moist cloth. The ammonia will wipe away any negative funk attached to the candle. Be sure to let your candles dry thoroughly before using them.

Bluestone and Laundry Bluing

Bluestone is a bright blue crystalline copper sulfate that was a popular ingredient in the Hoodoo olden days as an ingredient in floor washes for protection and to cleanse a space of evil spirits and negative energies. However, bluestone is highly toxic, and therefore it is no longer used. In its place, we find blue anil balls and laundry bluing.

One of my earliest memories as a very young child was the blue anil balls that someone in my home kept under my bed. I used to crawl under my bed and play with them. No one ever saw me do that, so no one told me not to. I assume they were there not for cleansing but for protection.

Blue anil balls and laundry bluing are used for gambling luck, spirit work, cleansing, protection, and whitening laundry. You can place blue anil balls anywhere in the home you feel needs cleansing—in the corners, under furniture, in closets or drawers. You can add them to mojo bags or jars of water to make blue water and set them in windows to thwart the evil eye and keep undesirables away. Or, add some laundry bluing to a bucket of hot water and detergent to make a nice, purifying floor wash.

Candles

Candles use the transformative power of fire to purify and provide necessary light to guide the spirits to the space in need of cleansing and blessing. Candles can function as calling cards to the spirits and saints in this way. It's important to note that when using any cleansing agent, you should also do some physical cleaning. If you live in perpetual clutter, you will have perpetual stagnation. Stagnation creates an environment ripe for meddling spirits to hang out and funk to begin to accumulate. So, your room should be cleaned before lighting your candle.

An easy way to cleanse and clear a space energetically is to light a white candle anointed with a conjure oil like Peaceful Home, Blessing Oil, or even plain olive oil in the center of the room in need of clearing. Say a prayer to the spirit of your choice, asking them to expel negative energy and turn stagnant energy into flowing energy again.

Another way to cleanse a room with a candle is to use the candle to petition a saint or Mama Mary. Light some rose or Peaceful Home incense and burn a blue candle for Our Lady of Lourdes (the Virgin Mary). Say, "In the name of the Father, Son, and the Holy Ghost, transform the evil into good and make my home peaceful again. Amen."

Eggs

Hoodoo and Latin American folk magic practitioners use eggs to clean people, places, and things. White eggs are used for general cleansings, while brown eggs are all-purpose. When black magic is suspected, eggs laid by black chickens are used.

A simple and effective way to spiritually cleanse your home with eggs is to use an egg for each corner of the room and go one room at a time. If your room has more than four corners, add an egg to each additional corner. Leave the eggs there for seven days. After the seventh day, remove and dispose of them in the trash outside.

Herbs and Incense

If you can't cleanse with ammonia, candles, or eggs, herbs and incense are fantastic options. Herbs burned for cleansing include lavender, lemon peel, cinnamon, palo santo, sandalwood, and rosemary. You can burn any incense as long as it is consistent with your intentions. Burn some of the dried herbs of your choice on a charcoal disc. Once you get a good smoke, pass your ritual tools through the smoke to cleanse them. As the smoke rises, it will take away the stagnant energy. This method is called *smoking*, and it is ideal for things that can't be cleansed in other ways. It can also be used as an adjunct to other methods.

Prayer and Song

Prayer, incantations, and words of power are potent ways to expel old energy and invite new energy into a space. Words are powerful because we must select them carefully and be fully mindful of our intentions as we state them out loud. I've used songs for years to cleanse and bless spaces. I usually smudge at the same time I am singing, because that is how I was taught to do it in the Native way.

Salt

Salt is an ideal cleansing agent because it absorbs negative energy. To make blessed salt, all you have to do is pray Psalm 23 over it. Then it is ready to be used in cleansings of ritual tools, spaces, and the body.

To cleanse a home using salt, fill a glass jar three-quarters full of water. Add half a cup of salt. Mix well until completely dissolved. Then, place the jar wherever you feel the energy is stagnant or negative. Don't place it where kids or animals can access it, because it needs to remain uncovered. Once in place, it is important not to touch it. The salt is there to absorb the negative energy. Leave it alone and watch what happens. You should see some crystallization develop as the water evaporates. When all the water has evaporated, dispose of the jar in the trash outside your home. Do not touch the crystals, as you will be contaminated with the funk it just absorbed for you. Repeat this process until your space feels open, fresh, and clear.

You can also make a cleansing floor sprinkle using salt. Combine salt, rue, and camphor and grind to a fine powder in a mortar and pestle. You can use this floor sprinkle in a couple of ways. One way is to sprinkle a little of the cleansing salt in the corners of each room after cleaning your floors with a vacuum, broom, or floor wash. The other way is to sprinkle it throughout your home all over the floors and allow it to sit for an odd number of minutes to absorb negativity. Then vacuum or sweep it up.

To cleanse ritual tools, fill a bowl with salt and lay your tool across the bowl on top of the salt. Leave it overnight. Wipe any salt off of the tool when you are finished. Toss the salt in the trash outside of your home.

Remember to remove all salt used for cleansing from your home. If used salt is left inside, arguments can start to happen between household members. Some say to throw the salt on the ground or under a tree, but I avoid doing that as the excess salt will kill the grass and anything living where you toss it. It is better to be aware of your environment and choose an eco-friendly alternative whenever possible.

Smudging

When thinking about smudging a space, our minds often go straight to sage, a Native American practice. But in Hoodoo and Conjure, any number of herbs and minerals are burned for cleansing, and they don't always smell as good as sage does (here's looking at you, asafoetida and sulfur). That's because a foul smell can expel foul energies.

To keep evil away, for instance, put three black chicken feathers in a fireproof bowl or plate. Add some ammonia, sprinkle with salt and cayenne pepper, and burn. Fumigate your home with this, and it will keep evil and people with evil intentions away from your home. Avoid inhaling the fumes.

A Note on the Indigenous Practice of Smudging

There is a lot of online chatter about non-Natives appropriating the use of sage. Some folks are saying not to use it unless you are Indigenous. I find that to be an overreaction by non-natives in an attempt to right something they have come to believe is wrong. Allow me to share an older Native perspective about this. Sage, and any other plant, does not belong to humans. It is our little sister, a relative, put on this earth by the Creator for our physical, spiritual, and emotional healing. It wasn't put here just for Indigenous cultures; it was put here for all of us. That said, not knowing how to use it correctly is what annoys me about non-Natives burning sage. Waving it around every which way, cursing, gossiping, and behaving irreverently while excessively burning it is not only cringe but also taboo. The act of smudging is a sacred ritual activity and should not be reduced to a flip-pant meme comparing it to Florida Water. Sage is among the four sacred Native plant medicines: cedar, sage, sweetgrass, and tobacco. The lack of reverence is off-putting, and this is what has caused such a stir, in my humble opinion.

In response to the "sage outrage," some folks have sug-gested exploring your culture of origin to find heritage herbs or practices for cleansing smoke or incense. I think this is a good idea and is consistent with the Red Road approach to healing. However, I do not believe one must limit oneself to only heri-tage traditions. In Hoodoo, the things burned are numerous and come from various cultures. The most important thing is to seek instruction on what you do not know and be respectful if you borrow from another culture's tradition.

Soap

Soap is an obvious cleansing agent for altar cloths, clothing, and other fabric types. The kind of soap used depends on what you are cleaning. I always opt for a mild Castile soap if ever in doubt.

I use soap fixed with a tiny amount of conjure oil to cleanse the rocks and sticks I find when hiking. For example, I use my Shaman's Stone Ritual Oil liquid soap when washing my found rocks. I use a soft toothbrush and gently scrub them to dislodge any dirt. Then, I carefully dry them with a white, lint-free cloth and allow them to air dry.

Sound

As mentioned in chapter 2, sound is a perfect agent for moving stagnant energy. To cleanse a specific object, first place it on your altar or some space large enough to move around it. Use your bell, rattle, instrument, bowl, or voice to create sound. Direct the sound to the object. The sound will change the molecules in the immediate area, causing them to move. In this way, any negative or stagnant energy in a space can be transmuted into positive, uplifting vibrations, completely transforming a home's mood, atmosphere, and ambience.

Sun and Moon

The sun and moon are excellent ways to cleanse and charge ritual items. Place your tools in front of a window where the sun shines or outside somewhere they will not be disturbed. To gain benefits from the sun, place them in the sun's path before noon and remove them before the moon rises. Then remove them promptly and store them safely.

Working with the moon's energies is a lengthier process. Considering the moon's phases, when it moves from the full moon to a new moon, it is ideal for cleansing because the moon is diminishing in appearance. Placing ritual tools under a waning moon helps eliminate stagnant negative energy. The phase from new moon to full moon is excellent for charging items since the moon is increasing in appearance. To both cleanse and charge ritual tools, leave them exposed to the moon for an entire lunar cycle.

Water, Holy Water, and Spiritual Colognes

In Voudou and Hoodoo, water simultaneously cleanses spiritually, energetically, and physically. It removes conditions and blesses and attracts people and energies. For example, a standard means for disposing of specific types of works is to toss the ritual remains into a moving body of water. Taking spiritual baths to remove hexes, unblock obstacles, remove and transform illnesses, and wash away grief are just some conditions for which water is used as a cleansing agent.

I always clean things like dishes, goblets, glasses, bones, and most stones with water before using anything else. However, water needs to be blessed before using it ritually. According to some beliefs, water can be made holy only if it is touched by a saint or blessed by someone with a high spiritual consciousness. Some believe water can be made holy by chanting the name of God over it or by adding blessed salt, holy ash, or holy earth to it. Once your water is blessed, you can use it as an ingredient in spiritual waters, floor washes, and ritual baths.

Spiritual colognes like Florida Water and Kananga Water are used as cleansing agents much in the same way water is. Like water, it should be blessed before use. Keep in mind that colognes contain a lot of alcohol, so they may not be conducive for cleaning items that could be damaged by alcohol.

A cool trick for cleansing with spiritual colognes is through an alchemical process of transforming the liquid into a cleansing fire. One of the ways Marie Laveau cleansed her candles—and other ritual items as well, I would suspect—was to pour a little cologne into a fireproof dish and light it with a match. It will ignite, bearing a pretty blue flame. You can then pass your ritual items through the blue flame so that the fire cleanses them. This technique is still practiced by some modern-day conjure workers.

HOODOO'S SHELLS AND STONES

The folklore associated with rocks and stones appears to have originated in antiquity. For example, Albertus Magnus asserted that opal brings joy to the heart of its owner and makes a person an object of love. Pagans dedicated sapphire to Apollo, making it a holy stone. Diamonds symbolized justice, constancy, and innocence, and, as a talisman, baffled sorcerers and destroyed poisons. Amethyst has long been a sobriety stone, while pearls are the crystallized tears of angels.

Unsurprisingly, people are attracted to the most beautiful and expensive crystals promoted in today's world of online magick. The traditional stones are a lot less exciting in appearance and seem to be suffering the cold shoulder of today's Instawitches and Twitches. Lodestones, thunderstones, fossils, cowry shells, coral, and conch shells have traditional magickal references to their mysteries. But if you are attracted to only sparkles and glitter, then the dull appearance of magnetite might not excite you. However, a highly magnetic lodestone should. Seeing the magnetic sand attach itself to a lodestone is pretty impressive, in my opinion. It shows how rocks and stones are alive with magnetism. Some practitioners suggest cleaning lodestones with Florida Water when first acquired, then allowing them to dry completely and adding magnetic sand to feed them.

Thunderstones are prehistoric hand axes or stone tools believed to possess occult power. Revered as sacred objects in New Orleans Voudou, they are used as amulets to protect people or buildings from lightning and other evils. Thunderstones are associated with Changó, the orisha of thunder, fire, and male virility, and Black Hawk, a Native American spirit guide served in Spiritualism and New Orleans Voudou.

Fossils are the preserved remains or traces of living organisms found in sedimentary, metamorphic, and volcanic rocks. Millions of years old, fossils are often used in New Orleans Voudou and Hoodoo as powerful talismans that can connect the practitioner with the spirits of the ancestors, to attract luck, increase personal power, and for protection. Fossils are also used in divination. Some of the most common fossils used in Voudou are coral, shark teeth, and bones.

Cowry shells represent wealth, fertility, protection, and spiritual connection. They are popularly used in divination, fetish-making, and worn as spiritual jewelry. Cowries are associated with the water spirits of Voudou, including Mami Wata and Yemaya, each revered in Voudou as the mother of all life.

Coral is a natural material produced by certain invertebrate marine animals and is worn by children and pregnant women as a protective amulet. It is also used to attract love, luck, and money; to enhance psychic abilities and spirit communication; and to protect against the evil eye. Coral is often associated with the element water and the planet Venus and can be used to balance emotions and heal the heart. Brain coral is specifically associated with mental acuity. Place a piece of brain coral on your altar for Crown of Success and King Solomon Wisdom works to achieve academic excellence, improve mental powers, enable wise decision-making, and enhance leadership qualities. Whisper Proverbs 1:5 to the brain coral prior to placing it on your altar to program it for ritual use: "A wise man will hear and will increase learning; and a man of understanding shall attain unto wise counsels."

Conch shells are the Voudou's communication device to the water spirits and are associated with the Voudou spirits Agwe and Olokun. Agwe is the loa of the sea, invoked by blowing a conch shell as a horn during rituals. Olokun is

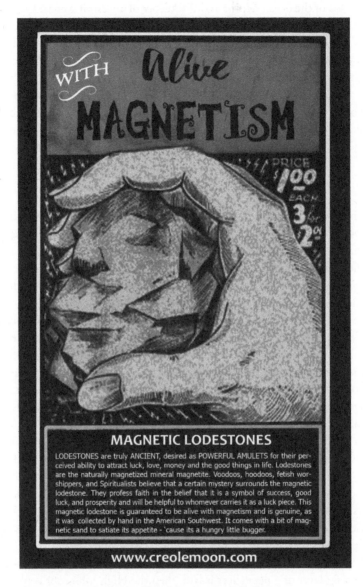

WITH *Alive*
MAGNETISM

PRICE
$1⁰⁰
EACH
3 for
$2⁰⁰

MAGNETIC LODESTONES

LODESTONES are truly ANCIENT, desired as POWERFUL AMULETS for their perceived ability to attract luck, love, money and the good things in life. Lodestones are the naturally magnetized mineral magnetite. Voodoos, hoodoos, fetish worshippers, and Spiritualists believe that a certain mystery surrounds the magnetic lodestone. They profess faith in the belief that it is a symbol of success, good luck, and prosperity and will be helpful to whomever carries it as a luck piece. This magnetic lodestone is guaranteed to be alive with magnetism and is genuine, as it was collected by hand in the American Southwest. It comes with a bit of magnetic sand to satiate its appetite - 'cause its a hungry little bugger.

www.creolemoon.com

Figure 6. Vintage-inspired label for magnetic lodestones.

the loa of the ocean depths and the keeper of ancestral secrets. Often depicted as a merman, Olokun is a powerful, mysterious spirit who rules over the realm of dreams, visions, and psychic abilities. His symbol is a conch shell filled with water, representing his vast knowledge and influence. Conch shells may be given as offerings to these and other water spirits.

Shells and coral may be cleaned with plain water and a soft toothbrush. Fossils may be cleaned with water as well, unless they are found in a soft shale or clay matrix. In this case, use a soft paintbrush to clean the specimen of debris.

TAKING CARE OF JOHNNY CONKER

The most popular root used in Conjure is High John the Conqueror root—*Ipomoea purga,* or jalap. There is a whole body of folklore behind this root that illustrates its significance in the lives of African Americans. High John the Conqueror is much more than just a root; it serves as a vessel to carry the spirit of the enslaved man, Johnny Conker, whose stories teach through the trickster paradigm.

High John the Conqueror is a master root in Hoodoo, Rootwork, and Conjure. It holds influence over all conditions. It is a flowering vine that overshadows all other plants for sunlight and sustenance. Traditionally, High John roots are anointed with Louisiana Van Van Oil and carried in the pocket as powerful amulets for drawing luck, personal mastery, power, sexual prowess, protection, and domination. It is said that the person who holds the High John root will be lucky in all things.

There are many ways to work with High John roots. Soak one in your favorite cologne to imbue it with its unique qualities. Use it in powder form as a sprinkling dust or incense. Carry one in a mojo bag or pocket for good luck. When the root is used as a charm, however, it requires feeding to retain its power. This practice reflects the belief that the indwelling spirit—John the Conqueror—must be nurtured to live. A typical spiritual meal consists of steel dust and sugar: one to attract, the other to sweeten.

Some folks keep their High John roots in a jar with ginger root slices. A bottom layer of ginger slices is laid, then the High John root is placed on top and covered with additional pieces of ginger root. The ginger is switched out annually to keep the energy on a high frequency. Maintaining a High John root this way keeps its power activated indefinitely.

Another way to keep your High John root happy and fed is to keep it in a bowl with magnetic sand, cinnamon, and sugar. Burn a green candle in front of it every week to keep it charged up.

To fix a High John root for sex, place it in a container with cayenne pepper and sugar. Take the root and put it under the bed of the person with whom you wish to have passionate sex. Keep that root on your person until you want to influence your partner's passion again. Then just put it under the bed each time you wish to make love.

TALISMANS AND AMULETS

Talismans and amulets are made from different materials, so it is necessary to adopt some general guidelines for their care. You can use cleaning products made specifically for each type of metal, but exercise caution and follow the directions on the product. For metal, use a soft polishing cloth made for jewelry. You can also wash talismans and amulets gently with warm water, mild soap, and a soft brush such as an artist's paintbrush or a new makeup brush.

Unless you are working with a particular talisman or amulet that requires charging it in the sunlight or exposing it to the elements, you should be careful with exposing your talismans and amulets to excessive heat and light. Stones such as amethyst and topaz can bleach, lose their color, or become damaged in other ways if left in the sun for too long. This damage does not typically happen while wearing them, but more so when left sitting in the sun for a time.

Be mindful of your talismans and amulets' exposure to chemicals. Beauty products like hairspray, perfume, and dry shampoos contain chemicals that can cause damage, so amulets and talismans should be covered or put away when you use these products. Also, if you swim in a pool that contains chlorine—as most do—the water can damage your amulets. Regular soap, dishwashing liquid, and other household cleaning products can also be damaging. It's a good rule of thumb to remove what dust and dirt you can before they come into contact with any of these elements.

Finally, be careful when you wear your talismans and amulets. They can be scratched, nicked, and broken simply by accident with everyday use. I have an issue when sleeping while wearing necklaces because they become tangled. I spend far too long trying to untangle them in the morning. I once broke a chain this way by accident. So, take a minute to remove your talismans and amulets before showering, swimming, sleeping, or bathing to minimize the potential for accidents.

TIGNONS

Back in 1786, the Louisiana Territory was under the Spanish rule of governor Esteban Rodríguez Miró. He was hell-bent on maintaining the racial status quo. He targeted women of color who were too light-skinned, "dressed too elegantly, or who competed too freely with white women for status" because they "threatened the social order."[17] He wanted a scarlet letter-level symbol to identify, subjugate, and shame the slave class.

Miró's solution was to enforce a law that forced Black women—free or not—to wear a headwrap called a tignon (pronounced *teen-yon*). They were to

Figure 7. A portrait of Marie Laveau by Frank Schneider (1920), based on an 1835 painting by George Catlin that has since been lost.

The Marie Laveau Voodoo Grimoire

cover their heads completely in the scarf to avoid offending white sensibilities. The law was intended to be oppressive but did not have the intended effect. In a testament to their resiliency and creativity, Black women turned their oppression into a fashion statement of resistance. They obeyed the law by covering their hair using scarves in bright, bold colors and patterns, getting creative with their knots, allowing small curls of hair to show, adding shells, feathers, and jewelry, and turning their tignons into beautiful fashion accessories. Before long white women noticed, and they began wearing tignons as well.

After the Louisiana Purchase, the tignon law was dropped, but women kept wearing them anyway. Today, Black women still wear beautiful tignons as fashion statements and to honor their ancestors.

Some say Marie Laveau wore a tignon, and some say she didn't. Some say she wore it only when she felt like it. One source, Blind Alexander, stated Marie Laveau belonged to the Society of the Ladies with Tignons.[18] Since she was born a free woman of color just two years before the Louisiana Purchase, she would not have been under the mandate. Nonetheless, the tignon endured as a fashion accessory long after it was law, and Marie Laveau is said to have worn one at least some of the time. The famous 1920 painting by Frank Schneider is believed to be of Marie Laveau wearing the iconic symbol of resistance.

Headwraps often require special care to keep looking fresh and clean. If you own and wear a tignon, you should care for it as the sacred garment it is. There are two ways to wash your headwraps and tignons: by washing machine and by hand.

When washing your headwraps using your washing machine, always use cold water and set it on the delicate cycle. Do not use bleach. To dry, shape them on a towel and allow them to air dry. You can also hang them up to dry, depending on the kind of headwrap you have. If your headwrap has elastic in it, do not dry it in the dryer because the dryer reduces the elasticity and will eventually cause it to break.

When handwashing your tignon, use cold water and a gentle fabric softener. Rub it gently in the solution. Avoid twisting. Place it on a rack or towel and allow it to air dry. This method helps your tignons and headwraps stay in excellent condition for as long as possible. Whichever method you use, say a silent prayer for your ancestors when washing your tignon.

PROPER STORAGE

Always store your ritual tools well. Keep your jewelry and amulets separate in soft velvet bags or arrange in a special jewelry box. Crystals can scratch if allowed to rub against each other, so be careful where you store them. Metal becomes tarnished when exposed to humidity, so rub your machete and knife blades with olive oil and keep them sheathed. Mojo bags tend to get dusty and brittle over time when exposed to the elements, so keep your gris gris in wooden boxes.

Taking care of your ritual tools is an excuse for shopping for gorgeous decorative boxes, bags, and containers. So go get some beautiful boxes for storing your beautiful ritual tools. Keep them out of direct sunlight in a cool, dry place, and they will serve you well for generations to come.

Chapter 5

CONJURE IN THE KITCHEN

I remember seeing Marie Laveau as a child. I was selling pralines for my mother, on St. Ann St. between Burgundy and Rampart, when this old woman who looked just like a ghost saw me and said, "allez petit" (French for "go away, child"). When I got home, I told my mother about this strange woman and she said, "child don't you ever stare at that woman, that was Marie Laveau."

—Unnamed informant, age 73

The Creole kitchen pantry in Marie Laveau's day would consist of meat, fish, greens, rice, grits, white potatoes, sweet potatoes, corn, turnips, eggplant, peanuts, okra, and homemade desserts. Leafy greens included spinach, collards, mustard, kale, and cabbage. Okra was the principal ingredient in gumbo and is believed to have spiritual and healthful properties. Traditionally, many elders would eat a large noon meal on Sunday after church consisting of Creole dishes like Hoppin' John, gumbo, jambalaya, fried porgies, and potlikker.

New Orleanians are known for their love of flavorful, spicy, savory foods. Many of our dishes begin with the Holy Trinity—onions, bell peppers, and celery. In contrast to the trinity is the classic French *mirepoix,* a base made up of onions, celery, and carrots, usually in a ratio of two parts onions, one part celery, and one part carrots. Mirepoix often serves as the starting point for a variety of stocks, soups, stews, and sauces.

The New Orleans Voudou spirits have their favorite foods. Some of their food offerings are simple, like fresh fruit, while others are elaborate, like gumbo. Much care goes into preparing the food as it is considered a magickal act. After the food is prepared, it is offered on the altar. After the ceremony, the food is shared amongst congregants while a portion is reserved for the spirits themselves.

The following is a collection of dishes in Creole cuisine that can be made as offerings to Marie Laveau, the ancestors, and other spirits of New Orleans Voudou. I have included dishes that are historically part of the Marie Laveau legend as her favorites. I have also included healthy dishes and recipes for the sick and infirm. Marie Laveau would have likely served some of these dishes while nursing her yellow fever patients back to health.

Whether you are a Voudouist or not, you will surely enjoy these tasty Creole dishes.

Figure 8. Old praline woman. From *The Romance of New Orleans,* published in 1919.

BLANC MANGE

Blanc Mange, meaning "white dish," has uncertain origins but was a mainstay in French cuisine in Marie Laveau's day. It was made and poured into a mold and then served cold, but it could also be served in a bowl like porridge. Blanc Mange was served on festive occasions and was even dyed different colors. It was also a mainstay as sustenance for the sick and infirm, as it is easily digested and filling.

> 1 quart milk, plus a little extra for mixing with the flour
> Sugar
> Rose water
> 4 tablespoons rice flour

Boil milk and season it to taste with sugar and rose water. Mix the rice flour with a little cold milk and add this to the other milk while it is boiling, stirring well. Let all simmer for about 15 minutes, stirring occasionally, until the mixture has thickened. Allow it to cool before consuming.

CONGRIS

Several stories claim to be the origin of congris, or red or black beans and rice, depending on who you talk to and where you are in the South. A dish typically credited to be Cuban in origin, it is likely traced to the slaves who brought the tradition of eating beans with them to the New World.

Red beans and rice were customarily prepared on Mondays in Louisiana, as this was the day for washing clothes during plantation days. A cauldron was kept over a low fire for washing throughout the day, making it convenient to slow-cook beans over the fire in a different cauldron alongside the clothes.

Congris was reportedly one of Marie Laveau's favorite dishes. According to some Spiritualists, congris is prepared on Sunday evenings as an offering to the powerful Indian spirit Black Hawk. Thus, it is commonly made by devotees as an offering to both spirits. Place a bowl of congris on Marie Laveau's altar and surround it with silver coins—nickels, dimes, quarters—and dollar bills. Place a bowl of red beans and rice with cornbread before Black Hawk's bucket. Annie Christmas also enjoys offerings of beans and rice.

Ingredients for Beans

> 1 cup dried small red kidney beans
> ½ small onion
> 1 red bell pepper
> 1 stalk celery
> 2 garlic cloves, peeled
> ½ teaspoon ground cumin

Ingredients for Rice

   1½ cups long-grain white rice, rinsed in cold water five times
   3 tablespoons olive oil
   2 cups chopped onions
   ¼ cup chopped red bell pepper
   2 garlic cloves, minced
   ½ teaspoon ground cumin
   ½ teaspoon dried oregano

Place kidney beans in a large bowl and cover with 3 inches of cold water for at least 4 hours or overnight. Drain.

Place 2 quarts of water, beans, onion, bell pepper, celery stalk, and garlic cloves in a large pot. Bring to a boil over medium-high heat. Reduce heat to medium, cover, and simmer until beans are tender, stirring occasionally, for about 50 minutes. Season to taste with salt. Drain, reserving the beans and bean-cooking liquid separately.

Bring 3 cups of bean-cooking liquid to a boil in a heavy medium-sized saucepan. Add rice; return to a boil. Reduce heat to medium-low, cover, and simmer until almost all liquid is absorbed, about 20 minutes. Uncover and fluff with a fork.

Heat oil in a heavy large skillet over medium-high heat. Add onions, bell pepper, garlic, cumin, and oregano and sauté until onions begin to brown, about 5 minutes. Add a half stick of butter. Stir in beans and rice; cook until heated, about 5 minutes. Season with salt and pepper. Yields 6 servings.

CREOLE CALAS

Calas are a type of puff pastry-like fritter made from leftover rice. Creole street vendors called "calas women" produced and sold these sweet pastries from baskets or bowls they carried on their heads. The *marchandes*, or street vendors, of old New Orleans included Marie Laveau's grandmother, Catherine Henry.

Calas are believed to be the brainchild of resourceful enslaved Africans brought to New Orleans from one of the rice-growing regions of Africa, such as Liberia, Ghana, or Sierra Leone. In the 1760s, when the Spanish took control of Louisiana, they introduced a legal mandate called *coartacion* that allowed slaves to name a price for their freedom. This limited the slave master's power, restricting them from continually raising the price of liberty. One way that enslaved African women raised money was by making and selling calas in the marketplace. More than fourteen hundred New Orleans slaves could buy their freedom under Spanish rule, though how many accomplished this by selling calas is unknown. We know Marie Laveau's great-grandmother was able to save enough money to purchase her freedom by working as a marchande. Could she have done so by selling calas?

There are a variety of recipes for calas. Here is one provided by a Creole woman in 1940 New Orleans named Remy Morand.

1 cup rice
½ cup sugar
½ yeast cake
1 cup flour
Confectioners' sugar

Cook rice to a soft creamy mush, add sugar and stir well. Dilute yeast in luke-warm water, add rice and sugar mixture, then stir in flour. Let batter set to rise overnight. Fry in oil or lard. Sprinkle with confectioners' sugar. Serve hot with cocoa or café au lait.

Figure 9. In 1990, Haydel's Bakery revived the old tradition of including miniature porcelain dolls with their king cakes. In 2010, the calas lady was the featured cultural icon.

CAFÉ AU LAIT

Café au lait is a popular beverage in New Orleans, where it is made with scalded milk and coffee mixed with chicory. The French developed a taste for this combination during their civil war when coffee was scarce, and chicory was added to enhance the flavor and texture of the brew. To make café au lait, brew some coffee and chicory and add an equal amount of scalded or steamed milk. It may be served in either a cup or a bowl.

> "Marie Laveau had a black woman living with her who sold peanuts, pralines, potato pones and I believe she sold powders and herbs. This woman went all through the French Quarter. I believe she directed people to Marie Laveau's house. Especially strangers. This woman was short and stout, she wore a tignon, a big figure dress, apron, and had a table to put her candles on."
>
> —Joseph Alfred, 85

CREOLE PRALINES

4 cups sugar
2 cans canned milk or cream
2 teaspoons vanilla
1 stick butter
Large bag pecans (whole or halves)

Put 1 cup of water in the freezer to test "doneness." Combine sugar, canned milk or cream, and vanilla in a saucepan. Cook for about 15 minutes on medium. Bring to a boil. Add butter. Keep stirring so the mixture doesn't boil over. After 45 minutes, drop some in the test water from the freezer. If it forms a ball, the candy is ready. Add pecans and stir for a few more minutes to cover the pecans. Grease a pan to put candy on when done. Drop by large spoonfuls onto the pan and allow to cool.

CREOLE SHRIMP BOGGED DOWN IN RICE

Here's an excellent Creole shrimp dish my mother used to serve. It is simple and relatively quick to make, but most of all, it is delicious! She called it Shrimp Bogged Down in Rice.

1½ cups uncooked rice
1 teaspoon salt
3 pounds fresh shrimp
Butter
½ teaspoon lemon juice
1 large onion
1 pod garlic
½ teaspoon lemon-pepper seasoning
⅛ teaspoon black pepper
½ teaspoon dried parsley, chopped

Cook rice in 3 cups boiling water and the salt. Boil gently without stirring for 15 minutes. Reduce heat to simmer while covered, about 5 to 10 minutes. Set aside. Peel and devein shrimp, wash well, and drain. Put butter in skillet with lemon juice and let melt. Add onion and garlic; sauté until soft. Add shrimp, lemon-pepper seasoning, and black pepper. Add parsley. Turn the shrimp until cooked. Pour this into cooked rice and toss gently.

HOPPIN' JOHN

According to lore, Hoppin' John was one of Marie Laveau's favorite dishes to make, eat, and serve to others. The main ingredient is black-eyed peas. Black-eyed peas, each possessing a spot resembling an eye, are said to protect from negativity and bad luck, especially in the form of the evil eye. On New Year's Day, many people make Hoppin' John and collard greens to ensure prosperity and abundance for the new year. Because black-eyed peas swell when soaked in water, they represent abundance, magickally speaking. The name Hoppin' John is thought to refer to the Southern folk hero, High John the Conqueror.

Interestingly, a silver dime is often cooked in Hoppin' John. The person who is served the dime is said to be especially lucky that year, and he or she will keep the dime as a lucky token throughout the year. In the South, our grandmothers often told us, "What you do on New Year's Day, you'll be doing all year." Therefore, we never wash clothes, do housework, or do anything else we don't want to be doing on a daily basis.

Here is a recipe for Hoppin' John that was handed down to me from my mother.

1 pound black-eyed peas
8 slices bacon, cut into fourths
1½ cups onions, finely chopped
1 cup celery, finely chopped
½ cup bell pepper, finely chopped
2 cloves garlic, minced
⅛ teaspoon Creole spice blend
⅛ teaspoon thyme
1 bay leaf
⅛ teaspoon rosemary
½ teaspoon salt
¼ teaspoon black pepper
2 cups cooked jasmine rice

Soak black-eyed peas overnight in water.

Fry bacon in a heavy skillet until crisp. Add onions, celery, and bell pepper and cook until the onions are transparent. Add 2½ quarts of water and bring to a boil. Add garlic, Creole spice blend, thyme, bay leaf, rosemary, salt, and pepper. Drain peas and add the boiling mixture. Barely simmer the mixture, partially covered, for 1½ hours. Add cooked rice. Serve with crisp French bread and butter.

MONEY GREENS

Greens are associated with attracting money; hence, the name *money greens*. Greens wilt and reduce a lot when cooked, so add more than you expect if you have never cooked greens before. Another thing is that some folks say greens tend to be bitter. If you pick them when they are young and tender, you won't have to worry about that. Furthermore, it's a little Creole secret to add a tablespoon of sugar to just about everything. That will take care of the slightest hint of bitterness.

½ cup olive oil
½ cup wheat flour
2 cups thinly sliced yellow onions
½ cup chopped celery
½ teaspoon salt
¼ teaspoon cayenne pepper
2 bay leaves

2 tablespoons chopped garlic

8 cups chicken stock

3 pounds ham hocks (about 4 medium-size hocks)

2 bunches each of collards, mustard, and turnip greens, thoroughly washed, picked over for blemished leaves, and tough stems removed (about 2¼ pounds)

1 cup spring water

Combine the oil and flour in an 8-quart pot over medium heat and stir with a wooden spoon until smooth. Cook the mixture, stirring constantly to make a blonde roux, for about 8 minutes.

Add the onions, celery, salt, cayenne, bay leaves, garlic, stock, and ham hocks. Bring the mixture to a boil, reduce heat to medium-low, and simmer, uncovered, until the hocks are very tender, about 2 hours.

Add the greens by the handful until they are combined in the mixture. They will wilt. Add 1 cup spring water. Simmer until the greens are very tender and the mixture is thick, about 45 minutes. Remove the bay leaves and serve warm. Yields 8 to 10 servings.

NEW ORLEANS GREEN GUMBO

This dish is adapted from the West African dish Palaver Sauce. During Holy Week, nine varieties of greens were cooked in a concoction known as *gumbo z'herbes*. Nine is a holy number for the Catholic Church, as it is the angelic number, reflecting the nine choirs of angels.

Interestingly, as it is called Green Gumbo, many of the ingredients are traditionally associated with wealth and prosperity. Cabbage has long been associated with good luck and abundance and is served as a stand-alone dish on New Year's Day and St. Patrick's Day in New Orleans to ensure good fortune throughout the year. Greens of all kinds are associated with money and wealth and are also a traditional dish for New Year's Day. Onions are associated with good luck—particularly red onions—while green onions bring good luck in finances, and white onions are a curative. Bay leaves are used for protection and luck, and cloves and allspice are common ingredients in money and good luck formulas.

Nine types of greens:

- Leaves of young cabbage
- Leaves of young radish

- Turnip greens
- Mustard greens
- Spinach
- Parsley
- Watercress
- Green onion
- Peppergrass

1 large smoked ham hock (optional)
6 tablespoons flour
4 tablespoons oil or shortening
1 large onion, chopped
1 bell pepper, chopped
3 ribs celery, chopped
1 tablespoon fresh parsley, chopped
2 bay leaves
4 sprigs fresh thyme
2 whole cloves
2 whole allspice berries
Salt and freshly ground black pepper to taste
Cayenne pepper to taste
6 cups cooked long-grain white rice

Wash all greens thoroughly and remove all stems or hard centers. Boil them all together in 1 gallon salted water with ham hock, if using, for about 2 hours. Strain the greens and reserve the water. Chop the greens finely and reserve. Make a brown roux of the flour and shortening in a large, heavy-bottomed stock pot. Add the Holy Trinity—onion, bell pepper, and celery—and sauté for 10 minutes. Add the chopped parsley and sauté 5 more minutes. Add the reserved cooking water, greens, herbs, spices, and seasonings. Simmer on low heat for 1 hour. Adjust seasoning as necessary.

Serve in large gumbo bowls. Put ½ cup of rice in each bowl and ladle generous quantities of gumbo over it. Optionally, you may season each bowl with gumbo filé. Yields 12 servings.

POTLIKKER

One of the healthiest natural dishes is potlikker, which refers to the leftover water from boiling green beans, or mustard, kale, collard, or turnip greens. Many of the nutrients are boiled out of greens when cooked, so the leftover broth—the potlikker—contains all of that goodness. Rather than throw it out, Creole cooks will save it and use it as a base for stews, soups, and gumbos. It can also be consumed by itself as a healthful tonic.

To make a nutritious pot of potlikker, you need to first boil some greens. To that end, get whatever greens are available in your local grocery store or garden and throw a pot of greens together.

1 cup diced bacon
1 smoked ham hock
1 Spanish onion, julienned
2 teaspoons red chili flakes
2 teaspoons sugar
2 pounds greens, sliced into thick strips
2 cups water or chicken stock

In a sauté pot, fry the bacon until crispy; add ham hock and onion. Sauté until onions are translucent. Add chili flakes, sugar, and greens. Sauté briefly, then add the water or stock. Cover and cook down over low heat until the greens are tender. You may need to add more liquid as necessary. Adjust seasoning to taste.

SPICY BOILED PEANUTS

Peanuts arrived in the South sometime during the eighteenth century on slave ships, which were frequently provisioned with them when preparing for the transatlantic voyage. Southerners started to eat them during the Civil War, when Confederate troops on the march to Georgia were split up and low on rations. Peanuts became a vital source of nutrition. The simplest way to make boiled peanuts is to cook them in a tall pot with lots of salt on a slow boil. But there are numerous spicier recipes, like the one below. Just throw everything in a pot, cover it with water and boil for ½ to 1 hour until tender. Bon appétit!

2 pounds raw peanuts
1 lemon, cut and squeezed
Bunch of celery salt

3 tablespoons chili powder
3 jalapeño peppers
5 cloves garlic
1 onion, quartered
1 tablespoon cumin
1 bottle liquid crab boil

If you decide to make some of these boiled peanuts, don't forget to offer a bowl to Baron Samedi, the Voudou spirit of Death. As peanuts are one of his favorite offerings, he would surely appreciate it! Boiled peanuts are also an excellent offering for Papa Legba, the Guardian of the Crossroads.

ST. JOHN'S BREAD

St. John's Bread is a wonderful traditional bread to make as an offering to St. John, Doctor John, and Marie Laveau on St. John's Eve. It's like a Catholic version of Indian frybread crossed with the famous New Orleans beignets. It is very delicious and worth making if you like baking the old-fashioned way.

1 tablespoon butter
1 tablespoon sugar
1 teaspoon salt
½ cup milk, scalded
½ cup boiling water
½ yeast cake dissolved in 2 tablespoons warm water
3 cups bread flour, sifted
Oil for frying

Combine butter, sugar, and salt in a large bowl. Add the milk and water and stir, then let cool. When lukewarm, add yeast and ½ cup flour. Mix thoroughly with a spoon, then add 1 cup flour. Continue to mix, adding the balance of flour gradually. Turn out on a floured board and knead until smooth and elastic. Return to a clean bowl, cover with a cloth, and let rise until double in bulk.

Turn out on floured board and roll to ⅛ inch in thickness. Cut in 2½ inch-wide strips and cut again to make squares or diamonds. Cover and let stand for 10 to 15 minutes. Fry in oil for about 4 minutes or until a delicate brown. Serve with maple syrup or milk sauce made by scalding 2 cups of milk in a double boiler to which 2 tablespoons of butter have been added. Serve hot.

SWEET POTATO PONE AND MAGICK
LAMP FOR ABUNDANCE

This recipe was brought from Barbados over two hundred years ago. Sweet potatoes are a traditional indigenous food representing abundance and good health. They are a nutrient-rich food that can boost vitality.

Before making this dish, make a simple magick lamp for abundance. On a flat wick, write your petition. Fill the lamp with olive oil, using a fireproof vessel as the container. Add a piece of raw sweet potato and some money herbs and curios to the oil. Place the wick in the lamp and light it. Once the flames ignite your petition, your request will be released to the universe to be acknowledged by the spirits. Keep the lamp burning in your kitchen to ensure abundance and good health.

Wash, peel, and grate the best quality sweet potatoes you can find. Measure 5 teacups grated sweet potato into a large bowl. Into this, stir 3 teacups of the best West India molasses, 2 teacups melted butter, 1 teacup preserved ginger cut into bits, 1 teacup preserved orange peel chopped small, 1 teaspoon salt, 1 tablespoon pounded ginger, and 2 tablespoons of the following spices: allspice, cloves, mace, and cinnamon. Mix everything thoroughly. Next, grease a plain cake pan, pour the pone in, and bake in a moderately hot oven; around 350 degrees will suffice. It should look dark and relatively clear when properly baked and like a dark, rich preserve. Insert a knife. When the blade comes out clean, it is done. Let it cool before taking it from the pan.

Let the first spoonful go to your ancestors as you spoon out that sweet goodness. Just set an extra plate at the table with the food. When you are done eating, put the food offering outside under a tree or a bush for the spirits to take away. You will be blessed with abundance in many forms so long as you remember your ancestors and keep that lamp lit for seven days at a time.

VOODOO CANDY

Voodoo candy, or bonbons, are small, round confections coated in chocolate. They were referred to as the "life of the party" back in the 1800s. According to the *New Orleans Times,* on November 11, 1867, a ball in the lower section of the city was so listless as to be dead—until, it is reported, a waiter served bonbons. After the partygoers consumed the bonbons, the affair became so frenzied and disorderly that the police had to be called in. Well, that sounds like fun—here's the recipe!

1 can sweetened condensed milk
¼ cup butter, melted
1 teaspoon vanilla
pinch of salt
2 pounds powdered sugar
2 12-ounce packages semisweet chocolate chips

Mix sweetened condensed milk, butter, vanilla, salt, and powdered sugar. Form into balls, place on a greased cookie sheet, and refrigerate until firm. Melt the packages of chocolate chips, dip the balls in the chocolate, and place on the cookie sheet. Refrigerate until the chocolate is hardened, at which point they are ready to eat.

WHITE TEA

This was a tea given to young children too young to consume regular green or black tea due to the caffeine content. They reportedly loved it. All you have to do is put 2 teaspoonfuls of sugar into a ½ cup of good milk and fill it to the top with boiling water. Stir and serve.

Chapter 6

CREOLE CURES
AND REMEDIES

Many of the better class of Creoles patronized Voudou in one form or another, whether to achieve results in love, business, or other affairs, but more especially for the purpose of relieving pain and sickness. Frotteuses—women who rubbed pain away—had power—that was always spoken of in whispers.

—Catherine Dillon, 1936

Back in the olden Plantation Hoodoo days, when anyone was sick, their condition was believed to be the result of being hoodooed. Likewise, when they recovered, it was thought the evil causing the disease had been exorcised and the bewitchment removed. Home remedies were always used to promote health and treat illness before summoning a doctor because wellness was believed to be the individual's personal responsibility. In addition, white man cures such as bloodletting and amputations went against their belief system and were resoundingly rejected. This holistic philosophy would guide Marie Laveau's healing and nursing efforts in the 1800s.

Studies of Creole folk healing cultures reveal individuals often utilize multiple avenues of healing to address health holistically. A proper diet, cleanliness, exercise, and sufficient rest are essential to maintaining optimal physical health. Prayer, healing rituals, and nourishing food are additional means of addressing illness from a traditional Creole perspective.

During Marie Laveau's lifetime, there were three major cultural influences on Creole medicine: African, European, and Native American. The use of prayers and charms, herbal medicine, and laying of hands were standard

Figure 10. Midwife going on a call, carrying her kit, near Siloam, Greene County, Georgia, 1941.

healing methods shared among each group. Marie Laveau is known to have utilized each of these healing modalities in her compassionate care of the sick.

In addition to different healing modalities, there are different categories of illness in the Creole worldview: natural, occult, and spiritual. There are important distinctions between them, as the illness category determines the treatment type. While natural causes primarily induce physical illness, occult causes may affect the patient's physical, psychological, and spiritual life.

Occult illnesses are a result of supernatural, rather than physical, causes. A sorcerer uses their powers and rituals to induce or ward off illness in a patient.

Spiritual affliction is the third type of illness. Spiritual illnesses result from willful violations of sacred beliefs and moral indiscretions such as adultery, theft, murder, and breaking taboos. In a word, it is God's punishment for living a sinful life. Preachers function as "spiritual doctors" that cure spiritual illnesses by utilizing the healing power of God. In contrast to conjurers and rootdoctors, spiritual leaders and preachers have limited knowledge of herbal medicine. Nonetheless, illness caused by spiritual dis-ease is considered natural because it is the will of God. Rootdoctors are well-equipped to treat all three types of illnesses.

Creole women were renowned for their healing knowledge and midwifery. Much of their expertise and cures appear without attribution in the various domestic receipt books. The remedies—presented by white physicians—are touted, bottled, and sold as "scientific combinations of medicinal ingredients that have the endorsement of the highest medical authority."[19] White physicians took the knowledge learned from Indigenous and Black healers and renamed simple plants with their scientific names, slapped them on labels, and made it appear as though their cures were new and based on superior white scientific knowledge. In fact, they used the same plant-based remedies rebranded with Latin names to impress the ignorant, further oppress Indigenous healers, and make money. In one popular medical receipt book, *Gunn's Domestic Medicine*, or *Poor Man's Friend*, Dr. Gunn makes the stunning admission "on consideration of the importance of this information, I will add a few more instances of the shameful impositions practiced on the mass of the people, by the quackeries connected with medical science." He then goes on to provide numerous examples, including *Oleum ricini*, meaning castor oil; *Oleum Terebinthinæ*, meaning the oil of turpentine; *Sal Nitre*, meaning saltpeter; *Sulphate Magnesia*, meaning Epsom salts; *Ruta Graveolens*, meaning common garden rue; and *Salvia officinalis*, the common sage plant.[20]

Folk remedies are often described as dangerous old wives' tales. Society has given the Food and Drug Administration the highest authority; if a treatment is not approved by that institution, it is considered unsafe and even criminal. Never mind all of the side effects accompanying every medication on modern-day pharmacy shelves.

That said, many cures based on folklore are ineffective. For example, a treatment for fainting spells involves making the patient smell their left shoe while rubbing their right hand. Or to cure spasms, one simply needs to pull off their clothes and burn them. Other remedies require gross ingredients and practices, like earthworm oil and boiling frogs. I have omitted such entries from this grimoire because they are ineffective and, thus, of no use to the modern practitioner.

Many Creole remedies rely on the healing properties of a single herbal ingredient. These single herb cures are called *simples.* Other remedies are multibotanical compounds. Most of the time, remedies consist of herbal medicine and prayer. In the past, some remedies were effective for reasons not related to the plant's actual medicinal qualities but to how behavior was affected upon using the plant. For example, the common herb asafoetida, a pungent, resin-like gum extracted from the taproot of several species of Ferula, was placed in a small bag and worn around the neck to prevent illness. If you have never smelled it, asafoetida comes by its colloquial names "stinky" and "devil's dung" honestly. The smell is so offensive, it keeps people from getting too close to one another, thus keeping harmful germs away. In addition, asafoetida is a part of Hoodoo's materia magica, as it is said to keep the law away and ward off evil and negativity. It can also be used to harm enemies. Medicinally, it is used for abdominal tumors and as a carminative, intestinal spasmodic, abortifacient, aphrodisiac, diuretic, sedative, and stimulant. It also aids indigestion and is a good source of antioxidants.

One of the most common ways of preparing Creole medicines is through herbal teas and tisanes. Tisanes are herbal infusions or decoctions from plants other than the traditional tea plant, *Camellia sinensis.* They are classified according to the part of the plant that is used. There are leaf, root, bark, flower, seed, and fruit tisanes. Herbal teas and tisanes are consumed for enjoyment as well as for their medicinal value.

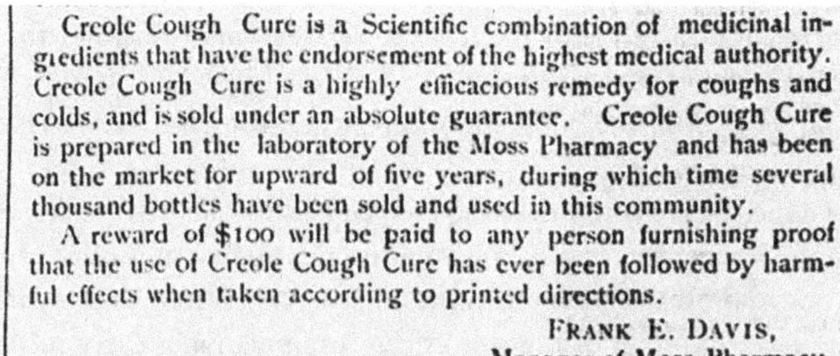
Creole Cough Cure is a Scientific combination of medicinal ingredients that have the endorsement of the highest medical authority. Creole Cough Cure is a highly efficacious remedy for coughs and colds, and is sold under an absolute guarantee. Creole Cough Cure is prepared in the laboratory of the Moss Pharmacy and has been on the market for upward of five years, during which time several thousand bottles have been sold and used in this community.

A reward of $100 will be paid to any person furnishing proof that the use of Creole Cough Cure has ever been followed by harmful effects when taken according to printed directions.

FRANK E. DAVIS,
Manager of Moss Pharmacy.

LAFAYETTE, LA., FEB 16th. 1899.

Figure 11. Nineteenth-century ad for Creole cough cure.

Following are some heritage cures and remedies of South Louisiana used in the nineteenth and twentieth centuries. Some of the plants used are the subject of modern scientific research, which is overwhelmingly yielding results in support of their efficacy. Creole healers like Marie Laveau would have availed themselves and their patients to remedies like these, along with diet, prayer, massage, and spiritual baths.

FOR MENTAL HEALTH

Several herbs are well known for managing chronic anxiety, stress, and anger. Catnip, calendula, and lemon balm are some of the best herbs for these conditions.

Catnip

Catnip (*Nepeta cataria*) belongs to the mint family and is quite aromatic. It is an herb you can use to help you chill and not feel so stressed out. In addition to helping with anger and anxiety, it can soothe an upset stomach. To use, you must make a tea to drink. The leaves and white flowers are used for this purpose, as the roots have a stimulating effect. Steep a handful of the fresh herb in hot water for 5 to 10 minutes. Sweeten to taste with honey if you like. You can use dried herbs or premade tea bags, as well. Catnip tea can be drunk several times a day if desired. Drowsiness is a common side effect of catnip tea, which is excellent for relaxation but not ideal for starting your day or going to work, so consider the time and your schedule when consuming. You should not drink catnip tea if you're pregnant, as it can cause uterine contractions that may result in premature labor. These uterine contractions can also cause a woman's period to start early.[21]

Calendula

Calendula (*Calendula officinalis*) is another well-known herb useful for the treatment of severe anxiety. In fact, one study found its use in the treatment of anxiety significant compared to Valium![22] The flower petals are used to make a tea. Steep 2 teaspoons in 1 cup of boiling water for 10 minutes, strain, and sweeten to taste. Note that the FDA considers calendula safe for general use. However, it may be best to avoid calendula while pregnant to reduce risk of miscarriage, given the herb's alleged effects on women's menstrual cycles. In addition, people taking sedatives or blood pressure medications may want to avoid it.

Lemon Balm

Lemon balm (*Melissa officinalis*) is a lemon-scented herb from the mint family. Traditionally, people use lemon balm to help improve mood and cognitive decline and decrease anxiety levels. In traditional medicine, people use lemon balm for various purposes, including digestive health and healing wounds. The leaves of this plant are also used to flavor foods. Due to its positive effects, many people consume lemon balm in tea form.

Tensyon Tea to Relieve Tension

To relieve tension, make what is called Tensyon tea by combining lemon balm, rosemary, Hawthorne, and soursop. *Tensyon* is Haitian Creole for "tension." For best results, allow the tea to brew for at least 10 minutes, then sweeten to taste and serve.

BURN REMEDIES

Natural burn remedies are best suited to treating first- and second-degree burns. Studies suggest that aloe vera, honey, and calendula may aid in the treatment of these types of burns.

Aloe vera has been used as a home remedy to speed up the healing of first- and second-degree burns for centuries.[23] My mother and grandmother always had aloe vera plants around the house, as do I. Nowadays, you can buy pure aloe gel at the store, but aloe vera is a plant you should have on hand if you have space for plants. It is easy to grow, and when you get a burn, all you have to do is slice off a leaf and squeeze the gel onto the burn area. You can feel the relief immediately, and it will stave off blisters and scarring. Apply directly to the wound area several times a day until it's finally healed. Keep the leaf in the refrigerator until you have used all the gel. The extra cooling from being in the fridge is an added bonus for pain relief. Aloe is an effective remedy for sunburn as well.

Honey is highly effective for burns.[24] Most research involves using raw, unprocessed honey covered by sterile gauze. Honey reduces infection and inflammation and, therefore, healing times. Because it is acidic, it can lower the pH of a burn, preventing bacterial growth. Manuka honey, in particular, is touted as an excellent remedy for burns. Though expensive, it is well known for its antimicrobial and anti-inflammatory properties. Whatever honey you use, be sure it is actually honey. Many brands selling honey are actually selling corn and sugar syrups with honey flavoring. You need actual honey to gain its benefits, so read the labels. I recommend buying local, organic, raw honey whenever possible.

Calendula is a flower that possesses anti-inflammatory properties. It is used in ointments, salves, and soaps as a soothing skin treatment. One study found that applying calendula extract to the skin promoted healing in rats with burn injuries.[25]

A heritage burn receipt consisted of a mixture of castor oil with the white of an egg for burns. The eggs are broken into a bowl after being passed over the burn area, then the castor oil is slowly poured in while the eggs are beaten. Enough oil is added to make a thick, creamy paste, which is applied to the burn. Leave the surface uncovered. The applications are repeated often enough to prevent their becoming dry or sticky.[26]

FOR COUGH, COLD, AND FLU

Herbs can be helpful for relieving the symptoms of cough, cold, and flu. Some common herbs that have antiviral, antibacterial, or anti-inflammatory properties are manglier, elderberry, mallow, ginger, mullein, horehound, honeysuckle, and sage. These herbs can be taken as teas, tinctures, and syrups.

For Flu

Boil 3 manglier roots (*Baccharis halimifolia L.,* aka groundsel tree, consumption weed). Reduce the liquid by half and add a good drink of whisky. Drink 3 cups without stopping. This comes from the notebook of a Cajun *traiteur* named Charles Bienvenu from St. Martinville, Louisiana, who collected a list of Native American curatives and lived to the ripe old age of one hundred and one.[27]

For Fever

A popular Creole folk remedy for fever is tea made from elderberry flowers (*Sambucus canadensis*). Add water, dried elderberries, and a cinnamon stick to a small saucepan and stir well. Heat the tea on high until it starts to boil. Then, turn it down to medium-low and simmer for 15 minutes. Allow it to cool for 5 minutes. Strain through a fine-mesh strainer into a mug and enjoy.

Grandma Bertha's Remedy for Hoarseness

In my grandmother's last years, she passed on all of her genealogy information to me, along with some recipe books. She chose to pass them on to me because I was the only one expressing an interest in our ancestors. Grandma Bertha was an excellent cook, and I was happy to receive the wonderful gifts she bestowed upon me.

As is common with books inherited, especially cookbooks and bibles, you can often find slips of paper or notes written in pen or pencil on special pages that our grandmothers placed there for reference. This particular remedy for hoarseness was found in the cookbook she passed on to me.

To treat hoarseness, combine 1 ounce of fine salt, 1 ounce borax, and 1 ounce baking soda and dissolve in 1 pint of water. To use, add 1 tablespoon of this mixture to 2 or 3 tablespoons of water and gargle.

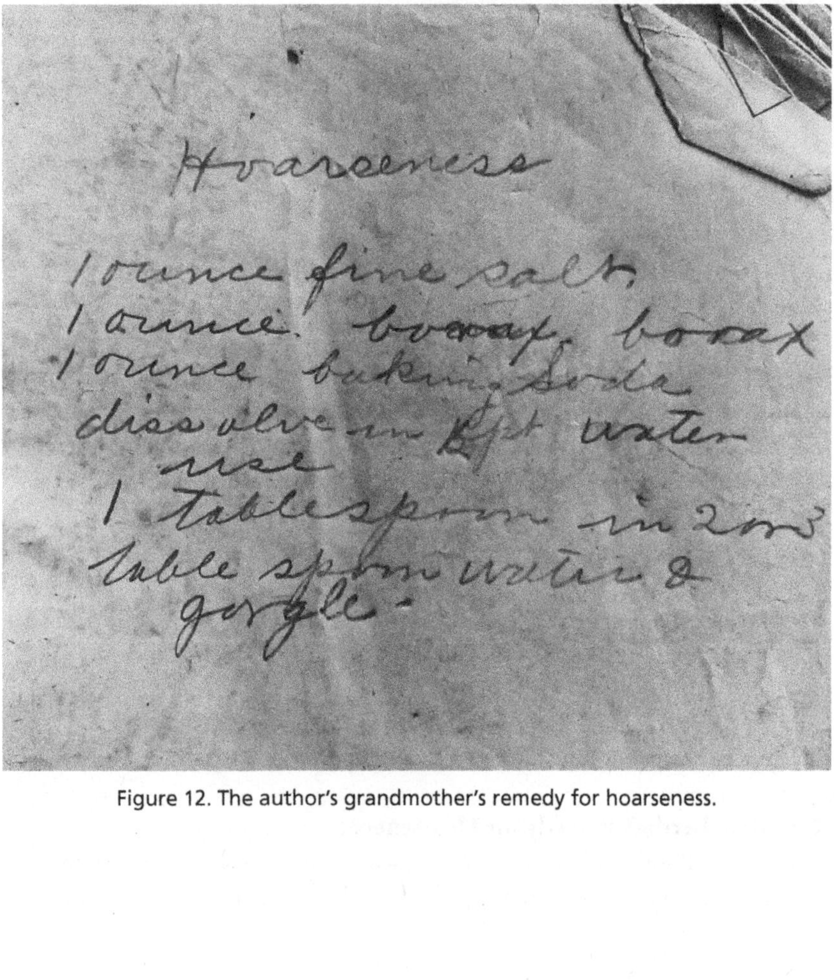
Hoarseness

1 ounce fine salt,
1 ounce borax
1 ounce baking soda
dissolve in 1 pt water
use
1 tablespoon in 2 or 3
table spoon water &
gargle.

Figure 12. The author's grandmother's remedy for hoarseness.

MEDICINAL HERBAL SYRUPS

Herbal syrups are a time-honored way to administer medicines to render them palatable. Syrups can be made with sugar or honey. Honey is preferable because it coats the throat and digestive membranes, is a natural preservative, and has a long shelf life. For proper preservation and a shelf-stable syrup, use a ratio of one part tea to one part honey. You can also use a lower sweetener-to-tea ratio, such as two to one or three to one, but if you do, you will need to use it quickly or refrigerate it. The best thing about sweet syrups is that, like teas and tinctures, you can formulate them using any combination of herbs.

It is best to use fresh herbs and berries when making your syrups. However, dried herbs and berries are readily available to most and may be used. If you use your herbs and berries in dried form, use twice as many dried herbs as fresh.

Brown Sugar Cough Syrup
This remedy is for coughs and sore throats. Combine brown sugar with a bit of water and cook down to syrup. Add lemons. Let lemons and sugar cook together. After cooking, add a nickel's worth of castor oil and a teaspoon of orange flower water. Mix with the sugar after it is cooked. Then, beat it until it is well mixed, and take a tablespoonful three times a day.

Common Cold Syrup
Make a syrup from mallow root (*Hibiscus lasiocarpus guimauve*) and drink it three times a day. This is a Creole folk remedy.[28]

Cough Syrup
Simmer together a handful each of mullein leaves and horehound in 1 quart of water, strain, and add 1 quart of molasses. Cook slowly until syrup is of good consistency.[29] Horehound can bring on menstruation and is an abortifacient so do not ingest while pregnant or breastfeeding.

Honeysuckle Remedy for Sore Throat
A reporter who once visited Marie Laveau's home caught a glimpse of honeysuckle vines through the door. He said they were "tenderly nursed for their fragrance" and used "as a Creole remedy for sore throat." Indeed, honeysuckle is widely known for its medicinal benefits, and the taste is very sweet. You can mix up a batch of this medicinal honeysuckle-infused honey for use in treating

sore throats. It keeps in the fridge for up to one month, but you can freeze some in ice trays to get you through the winter months as well.

>   2 cups fresh, wild honeysuckle flowers
>   1 quart water
>   1 cup local honey

Gather 2 cups of fresh honeysuckle blossoms. Be careful to retain the stamen, where the nectar resides. In a small pot, bring 1 quart of water to a boil, then add the honeysuckle flowers. Stir to make sure all flowers are immersed. Turn the heat down to low and simmer for 10 minutes. Strain off flowers and return liquid to pot. Bring the liquid back up to a boil and stir in 1 cup of honey. Continue to boil for 1 minute, then remove from heat and allow to cool before storing.

To use, add 1 to 2 teaspoons of honeysuckle syrup to a warm tea to sip or take 1 to 2 teaspoons at a time every 2 hours, as needed. Do not administer to children under two years old.

Sage Tea for Colds

Brew some of this medicinal herbal tea for colds and upper respiratory ailments.

>   ½ ounce dried sage
>   1 quart spring or distilled water

Bring water to a boil and remove from heat. Add the sage. Infuse for half an hour and then strain. Lemon and honey may be added to counter the bitter taste. Avoid drinking sage while pregnant as some varieties contain thujone, which can bring on menstruation and possibly cause a miscarriage.[30]

DIGESTIVE HEALTH

Herbs can be beneficial for digestive health in various ways. For example, ginger, chamomile, and peppermint are effective remedies for bloating, indigestion, and nausea, while dandelion and fennel are known to support liver function. Here are two herbal receipts to help with nausea and heartburn.

Agrimony Antacid

Agrimony is an herb that has been used for centuries to treat various ailments, including indigestion, diarrhea, and sore throat. It contains compounds that may have anti-inflammatory and antioxidant effects. Likewise, alfalfa controls stomach acidity because it is an alkaline herb. It can effectively control the stomach's pH levels, while oak bark is known for its anti-inflammatory properties, which makes it helpful for heartburn.

    1 cup fresh agrimony leaves
    ½ cup alfalfa leaves
    ¼ cup oak bark
    3 cups red wine

Macerate the crushed herbs in red wine for 1 month. Strain. Drink 2 tablespoons three times daily to eliminate stomach hyperacidity. Do not ingest if pregnant or breastfeeding.

Ti-Baum Tea for Digestion

A common tea used to strengthen the immune system and help with digestion is called *ti-baum* tea, meaning "mint" in Creole. It is used for stomach cramps and inflammation. Steep a handful of fresh mint leaves in a cup of hot water, sweeten to taste, and serve to anyone with a tummy ache for quick relief. Dried leaves may be used in the absence of fresh ones.

FOR ORAL HEALTH

In addition to practicing good oral hygiene habits like brushing, flossing, and dental check-ups, you can employ natural remedies to treat common dental problems. For example, chewing on a sprig of parsley or mint is excellent as a quick remedy for bad breath. Here are a couple of other simple and safe remedies.

For the Teeth

Take a pint of spring water and add 6 spoonfuls of the best brandy to it. Wash the mouth often with it, and in the morning roll a bit of alum around in the mouth. Do not swallow. This remedy will rinse away any food particles, bacteria, or plaque that remain after brushing.

For a Toothache

Apply essence of peppermint above the aching tooth. Essence of peppermint is a highly concentrated form of peppermint essential oil in alcohol. This remedy is effective because peppermint contains menthol, which has antibacterial properties and is a natural numbing agent.

FOR SWELLING AND INFLAMMATION

Swelling and inflammation cause pain, stiffness, and reduced mobility and are symptomatic of various health conditions like arthritis, infections, sprains, and strains. Nonsteroidal anti-inflammatory drugs (NSAIDs) like ibuprofen and aspirin are the most common modern medications for such conditions. But they also have adverse side effects and may be contraindicated for use with other medications. NSAIDs, for example, are well-known for their nasty side effects that range from stomach upset to liver damage. Our ancestors did not have to worry about such side effects in the past because their remedies preceded big pharma and only included minimal ingredients, massage therapy, and topical treatments. Thus, Marie Laveau used rubdowns, herbal teas, and poultices to treat these common ailments. Following are a few of her likely remedies for swelling and inflammation.

To Cure Swelling

According to Old Man George Nelson, if a person went to Marie Laveau with a swelling of some sort, she would tell them to go to the drugstore and get a box of Epsom salts, a bottle of alcohol, and a box of cream of tartar. She would rub them down with this mixture three times a day and pray at the hours of nine, twelve, and three o'clock. This remedy, he said, would get rid of the condition right away.[31]

Haitian Ginger Tea

Ginger tea has a host of medicinal and health benefits. It boosts the immune system; reduces inflammation, stress, and nausea; enhances digestion; improves blood circulation; and relieves menstrual discomfort. To make Haitian Ginger Tea, wash off a ginger root, peel the skin off, and slice it into several small pieces. Place the pieces into a small cooking pot, add water, cinnamon, star anise, and stir. Bring the mixture to a boil and allow to boil for 5 minutes. Reduce to a simmer and allow to cook for 5 more minutes. Pour the mixture through a strainer into a cup and add brown sugar to sweeten.

For Inflammation

A poultice is a healing paste spread on a warm, moist cloth and applied to the body to relieve inflammation and promote healing. It can be made from different healing herbs, plants, clay, mud, salt, or charcoal wetted with water or other fluids. Elderberry leaves (*Sambucus canadensis*), prickly pear cactus, and bristle mallow (*Modiola carolinianamauve*) can help with inflammation. To make a poultice, mash the fresh or dried plants with water to form a paste, apply it directly to the inflamed area, and secure it with a bandage or tape. You should leave the poultice on the skin for several hours or overnight, and change it as needed.[32]

MISCELLANEOUS CONDITIONS

There are many health remedies that do not fit into a specific category. These remedies may benefit different conditions, such as relieving headaches and improving virility, and employ techniques such as cure-alls, oils, and prayer. Following is a selection of remedies using different techniques for miscellaneous conditions.

A Cure-All

Most, if not all, folk medicine traditions have what is called the cure-all. In Hoodoo, the cure-all was very popular amongst practitioners. It was a spell that could solve all problems. There were different cure-all recipes; one was mixing jimson weed with sulfur and honey. This potion was placed in a glass, rubbed against a black cat, and then slowly sipped.

Cure-alls vary from culture to culture. For Caribbean Creole cultures, a cure-all is a plant called cerasee. Cerasee is a wild variety of *Momordica charantia* or bitter melon plant. It is used medicinally for all sorts of ailments. It has detoxifying effects when consumed and is used for high blood pressure, diabetes, and constipation.[33] It also has anti-inflammatory and analgesic properties, making it a good pain reliever. Because it looks like a weed, it tends to be overlooked as a plant with medicinal properties.

The most common way to prepare cerasee is to make it into a tea. Harvest a few handfuls and wash them with water. Throw all of it in a pot of boiling water—stems and all. Simmer until the water turns green. Cerasee is a bitter herb, so you may want to add a little honey to sweeten it. Cerasee is also sold prepackaged in grocery and natural food stores.

For Headache

This old cure for getting rid of a headache comes from the notebook of Cajun *traiteur* Charles Bienvenu. Take some sweet gum leaves and put them in a vase. Pour some warm water into the vase to wilt them. Then, press them together, encircle the head with them, and cover them with a clean cloth.[34]

To Increase Sexual Stamina

This simple herbal tea showcases Marie Laveau's skill as a rootdoctor. It also gives us a little insight into how she likely addressed both the physical and spiritual aspects of a condition. She had the knowledge and the common sense to ask the right questions to determine whether the solution to a sexual potency problem should be medicinal, magickal, or both. This tea seems to be a dual medicinal/magickal formula and is allegedly one of Marie Laveau's favorite recipes.

A spell for male virility is made as a medicinal conjure. To increase sexual stamina and to add potency to a love working, the patient is instructed to chew on a piece of snake root 9 times and drop it into a cup of rose hip tea. Then, the tea is drunk either by itself as a self-intervention or combined with another love working for which there is the same goal. For example, if you are burning a candle to light your sex life on fire, you can drink the tea at the same time to enhance the spell. Fridays and full and waxing moons are particularly effective witchy times for love magic.

Know Your Roots

As a word of caution, when you run across recipes that involve roots for which there is more than one type with the same common name, it is incumbent upon you as a conjure worker to know the difference between them. For example, Sampson snakeroot (*Psoralea psoralioides*) is used for male virility (enhancing a man's nature) and love, whereas Seneca snakeroot (*Polygala senega*) is used for protection against snake bites and evil energies of all kinds. Medicinally, seneca snakeroot is used to increase lactation. On the other hand, black snakeroot, also known as black cohosh, is used as protection against unwanted illness, evil, and harm. Also—and this underscores the importance of knowing your roots—black snakeroot is used to send an unwanted lover packing and as a general banishing agent.

Imagine if you did not know this and you used black snakeroot in making the above tea instead of Sampson snakeroot!

Furthermore, black snakeroot has specific medicinal properties, so you wouldn't want to just drink it willy-nilly. Black snakeroot is used to treat symptoms of menopause, premenstrual syndrome (PMS), painful menstruation, acne, and osteoporosis, and for starting labor in pregnant women.[35] As you can see, it is used for women's health issues. Any time you ingest an herb, either through eating it, drinking a tea, or smoking it, you must consider it a medicine. You are responsible for learning what it is used for and what the contraindications may be.

A Rare Green Oil for Aches and Bruises

Take 2 quarts of olive oil and pour into a larger container. Take 4 handfuls each of wormwood, sage, southernwood, and chamomile plus ½ gallon of red rose buds from which the white is cut and tear them crudely together. Add to the olive oil. Once a day for 9 days, stir well. Then add 4 handfuls of lavender tops to the mixture and blend well. Allow to stand for 3 or 4 more days. Cover tightly and boil on a low fire, stirring often. Add a half cup of brandy and let it boil an hour more. Then strain the liquid through a coarse cloth and let stand until cold. Stir in glass containers. Warm a little in a spoon or saucer and apply to the affected area.

For a Safe Pregnancy

Tie a blue or white handkerchief around a statue of Our Lady of La Leche and pray a novena offering a blue or white candle daily for 9 days. Anoint the handkerchief by drawing three crosses on it using blessed olive oil. Each day, lay it across your abdomen and pray three Hail Marys.

Soothing Joint Formula

Here is a recipe for a mentholated ointment to help relieve aches and pains.

> 1 cup sesame seed oil
> 1 tablespoon menthol crystals
> 2/3 cup avocado butter
> 10 drops eucalyptus essential oil
> 3 drops lemon essential oil

Combine the sesame seed oil and menthol crystals over a double boiler and heat until the crystals melt. Remove from heat and mix in avocado butter and essential oils. Stir and pour into jars. Apply to achy knees, lower back, or other joints. The eucalyptus and lemon oils combined with the highly scented menthol crystals work great together.

Sting-Healing Ointment

> 1 pound petroleum jelly
> 4 teaspoons dried agrimony leaves
> 4 teaspoons dried marigold leaves

Melt petroleum jelly in a double boiler. Stir in the herbs and heat for 2 hours, until the herbs begin to get crispy. Strain by pouring through cheesecloth. Squeeze the cloth to release all the liquid. While warm, pour the ointment into clean glass containers. Use as needed.

To Treat Asthma

The therapeutic inhalation of smoke and vapors was a predominant treatment of choice for a variety of illnesses since antiquity in most Western and Eastern medical traditions, including Ayurvedic, Egyptian, Greek, and Native American medicine. Throughout the 1800s, the therapeutic inhalation of *Datura stramonium* was enthusiastically adopted by asthmatic patients and their physicians largely for its antispasmodic properties.[36] For example, the *Confederate Receipt Book* provided this remedy for asthma:

> Take the leaves of the stramonium (or Jamestown weed), dried in
> the shade, saturated with a pretty strong solution of salt petre, and
> smoke it so as to inhale the fumes. It may strangle at first if taken

too freely, but it will loosen the phlegm in the lungs. The leaves should be gathered before frost.[37]

The Cherokee were known to employ smoking *Datura stramonium* for the treatment of asthma,[38] and the Cahuilla steamed the leaves of *Datura wrightii Regel* and inhaled the therapeutic vapor in the treatment of severe bronchial and nasal congestion. The Cahuilla also carried vials of sacred thorn apple (*Datura wrightii Regel*) as a charm for good luck.[39]

Figure 13. Burning an herb bundle.

Chapter 7

INCENSE

I lived right down in the heart of what they called Hoodoo land, in the same block as Marie Laveau. She was a Hoodoo queen and was nice and good and did lots of charity work. I was between 9 and 11 then and used to run errands for her. She sent me to the drug store to buy bergamot and incense powders.

—Cecile Hunt, 1940

Incense has always had a solid connection to both religious rituals and the profession of healing. In the earliest known Egyptian therapeutic procedures, for example, patients were exposed to incense smoke for treatment. During the yellow fever outbreak in New Orleans throughout the 1800s, people burned copious amounts of tar and sulfur to purify the air and prevent infection. Incense also creates an ambiance conducive to ritual activities. Incense is integral to New Orleans Voudou thanks to the Catholic Church and Marie Laveau, who enjoyed burning it in her cast iron pot and charcoal brazier during her ceremonies. It is clear she considered incense a fundamental part of her Voudou practice.

There are several ways to reap the benefits of incense and the ashes it leaves behind. There are rituals done with incense combined with psalms and prayers, and you can even set up an incense altar to perform simple yet powerful workings.

THE INCENSE ALTAR

Your incense altar should be facing east or the rising sun. You need a flat surface that is a defined space. It can be a small table, dresser top, mantle, flat rock on the floor, or even outside. The altar should be baptized before use. To do this, burn frankincense, and say three Our Fathers and seven Hail Marys. Anoint the altar with Holy Oil, then sprinkle the altar with holy water and say, "I baptize you in the name of the Father, Son, and Holy Ghost. Amen."

Your incense altar should have a candle on it to light before burning incense. The candle can be a white glass-encased candle, chime, votive, or even a tea light. Lighting the candle activates the altar.

In addition to a candle, you need an incense burner. You can even offer flowers to your altar if you desire.

CREATE AN INCENSE BOWL

The incense bowl holds the ash or sand base upon which your incense burns. I recommend a brass bowl for this purpose, as brass is ideal for burning incense. You can also use a small iron cauldron for burning incense, or another fireproof container, if you prefer. Whatever you use, it should be large enough to catch the ashes that drop and allow them to accumulate. Bonus points for a burner with three or four legs lifting it from the surface it sits on.

The two most common bases upon which to burn incense are sand or ash. If you are using sand, make sure it is at least one or two inches deep in your bowl or burner. Then you can either insert incense sticks in the sand without worrying about them falling or place charcoal disks on the sand without worrying about the bottom getting too hot and burning the surface underneath.

I use both sand and ash, depending on my end goal. But I do not mix the two. I also use dirt, as well. I always use the law of correspondences to decide which kind of sand, dirt, or ash I use. For example, I might use dirt from a bank or casino if I am burning incense to draw money. If burning incense to honor my ancestors, I might use sand from the Gulf Coast or dirt from the jungles of Costa Rica.

To create your ash base upon which to burn fresh incense, you must prepare the ashes. Your final product should be ashes that are smooth and silky. Incense ash will contain not only ashes but also unburnt nibs and charred resin pieces, so you will need to pick these out of the ashes using a pair of tweezers. Save the unburnt nibs in a glass jar to burn at a later date. You should regularly attend to your incense bowl to keep it clean and fresh. Once you have picked out the nibs and unburned or burnt resin pieces, you can sift the ash using a sieve and keep it to either refill your incense bowl or start a new one. Stir the incense ash with the tweezers to aerate the ashes, and gently shake or tap the bowl on a hard surface to level them. The ash should be light and airy and free of nibs. To finish the incense bowl, use a flattened spoon to tamp down and smooth the ash.

Be careful not to pack the ash too hard. There is a tendency for witchlings to overwork the ash and end up with a base that is too compact. With a bit of patience and a lot of practice, you can create a very smooth surface so that when you offer a stick of incense, it drops effortlessly into the ash. The end goal is a softly packed foundation about two inches thick.

I save all incense ash to reuse in a variety of ways. You can add ashes to sachet powders and conjure dusts, and use them to make amparos. You can also incorporate incense ashes into conjure clays for making doll babies. Unless you are reusing the ash as a base for burning more incense, be sure the ashes you save to reuse are from workings of a similar nature. For example, you don't want ashes from a stop gossip working to meld with a love working.

CHARCOAL DISCS

Resins do not always burn easily on their own, so it is customary to place them on a charcoal disc. You can also place self-lighting incense on a charcoal disc to get it started. Special charcoal discs are made for this purpose, and most incense outlets carry them.

Hold the charcoal away from your fingers using a tong. Light it with a match or lighter and watch the tiny sparks ignite. You will see it catch and sizzle, indicating the charcoal is spreading across the surface. Place the disc on the ash or sand in your incense bowl with the glowing side up. Now you can drop herbs, self-lighting incense, herbal powders, and resin incense onto it.

Do not use self-lighting charcoal briquettes made for barbecue as incense charcoal, as it produces toxic fumes.

TYPES OF INCENSE

There are several different types of incense: stick, resin, powdered, cone, self-lighting, and aromatic woods. Stick incense is practical and quick to light and use. All you have to do is place the stick in the incense burner or bowl and light it. Resin incense refers to the gums and resins excreted from trees. It is incense in its purest, most natural form. Frankincense, myrrh, copal, pine resin, storax, benzoin, rock rose, and dragon's blood are examples of resin incense. This type of incense needs to be burned on charcoal.

Self-lighting, powdered incense has always been a core activity for hoodoos and Spiritualists. It consists of loose, powdered herbs, resins, and woods (90 percent) mixed with saltpeter (10 percent). It is then sprinkled over a charcoal disc or poured into a little pile and lit directly.

Aromatic woods are fragrant woods burned as incense. Palo santo, sandalwood, and cedarwood are examples of aromatic woods used as incense. They can be burned in stick form, chips, or powder. Cedar wood and sandalwood often form the base for other incense formulas.

For lots of smoke, leave your charcoal discs with incense burning uncovered. If you would prefer little to no smoke, you can cover the incense with a layer of ashes. This technique allows you the benefits of the fragrance without the potential irritant of the smoke.

The formulas in this chapter are for some of the more popular incense formulas used in Hoodoo, Voudou, and Conjure. Some are made into powders, while others may be loose leaves or a blend of gum resins. Precise measurements are not given, as they never are in Hoodoo and Conjure. Making formulas is an intuitive process; you need to feel out the formulas and experiment with them to make them your own. The incense will need to be burned on charcoal discs.

In keeping with my promise to make this grimoire contain simple yet potent formulas, I have provided recipes that consist of just three to four ingredients. You will find the ratio of plant to resin in each formula given. Formulas with three to four ingredients are easy to replicate if you have a good supply of herbs and resins on hand. If you decide to venture out on your own and create your own formulas, you will find a good rule of thumb is to combine two herbs and a resin to be an ideal ratio. You can also add wood to the mix, or one herb, one wood, and one resin to make a nice blend that burns well on charcoal. Whatever your final formula is, it should contain an odd number of ingredients.

Conjure oils and essential oils may be added to incense mixtures, especially when the recipe calls for an herb that doesn't smell good when burned. Essential oils can enhance the fragrance of the incense, but they can also make it more flammable, so be careful with your ratios. The added oil should dampen the incense slightly but not saturate it. One good example of a fantastic smelling herb in the raw that smells bad when burned is mint. When incense recipes call for it, I will add the essential oil instead of the plant material and get a satisfactory result. Knowing when such substitutes can be made comes with time and experience.

For each formula that follows, a description of its purpose is provided, as is a list of ingredients and suggestions for its ritual use. You will learn some tricks for one formula you may want to use with another, which is perfectly fine. A common practice with incense rituals is to write a simple petition and place it under the incense burner prior to lighting the incense. Another practice is to write out a petition or prayer, five-spot it with a conjure or essential oil, tear the paper up into tiny pieces, add it to the incense blend, and then burn it.[40] Unless otherwise stated, compound the ingredients for each formula in a mortar and pestle or coffee grinder until well blended. To burn, place a pinch or two on a charcoal disc.

Adam and Eve Incense

Adam and Eve is an attraction formula designed for soulmates and may be used by any gender when the goal is to strengthen the love between two people. It is an excellent love-drawing incense, and the aroma is said by believers to bring your lover back to you if you have drifted apart or fought.

Dried apple peels
Balm of Gilead buds
Rose petals
Dried cloves
Myrrh

On a piece of parchment paper, write down the names of the two lovers to be charmed using Dove's Blood Ink and draw a heart around both names. Dove's Blood Ink is a magical ink used for writing spells, sigils, and seals. It is believed to have a powerful effect on love, peace, and reconciliation. Despite its name, Dove's Blood Ink does not contain any actual blood from doves or any other animals. It is usually made from natural ingredients such as red wine, dragon's blood resin, and cinnamon. For extra strength to the ritual, anoint the corners of the paper with Adam and Eve Oil.

Place the parchment square under the incense burner, then light the incense to create an enduring bond that is impossible to break. When the incense is done burning, burn the parchment paper, saving the ashes and placing them into a red flannel bag along with some apple seeds, cloves, myrrh, and rose petals. The bag should be carried close to the heart by one of the two lovers. If both partners are participating in the ritual, then you can make two mojo bags and have each person carry their mojo bag near their heart.

African Ju Ju Incense

This incense is burned in conjunction with crossing, hexing, and protection works. It is also used for psychic development. To make it, grind the frankincense into a powder and blend with the other powders. To burn, place a pinch or two on a charcoal disc.

Frankincense
Galangal powder
Vetiver root powder

This work is a technique that can be employed with any incense ritual. To protect someone, write the person's name along with the protection you want the person to receive on a piece of parchment paper. Anoint each corner and the center of the paper with African Ju Ju Oil or Protection Oil. Tear the petition paper into tiny pieces, mix it with the incense, and burn on charcoal.

Algiers Fast Luck Incense

Algiers Fast Luck is decidedly New Orleans in origin and is a triple luck success formula used for quick success in gambling luck, love, and sex. Blend the cinnamon and nutmeg powders well and add the wintergreen oil sparingly as it has a tendency to overpower other scents.

Cinnamon powder
Nutmeg powder
Wintergreen essential oil

Before playing any games of chance, be it cards, dice, bingo, or the lottery, place a representation of the game under the incense burner. You can use an actual deck of cards, a photo, or the name of the horse you want to win. Then, burn the incense before engaging in any gambling activity.

All Saints Incense

This incense is a potent formula for healing, success, and uncrossing rituals. It is used when you need intercession from the highest spirits. It can also be used on the Feast of All Saints, November 1.

Lavender flowers
Vetiver
Mugwort

Write your petition on paper and place it beneath the burner. Light the incense and pray with confidence that your petition will be heard:

Almighty ever-living God, by whose gift we venerate in one celebration the merits of all the Saints, bestow on us, we pray, through the prayers of so many intercessors, an abundance of the reconciliation with you for which we earnestly long. Through our Lord Jesus Christ, your Son, who lives and reigns with you in the unity of the Holy Spirit, God, for ever and ever. Amen.

Altar Incense

Altar incense is a holy incense formulated to attract sacred, beneficial spirits to the altar and to open and close rituals. New Orleans practitioners use this incense along with Holy Spirit and Louisiana Van Van when doing healing magick and communing with the saints and spirits.

Frankincense
Myrrh
Cinnamon

Burn as a general incense on your altar to cleanse and purify the area. Use as an aid to meditation and prayer.

Angel Incense

Angel incense is designed for protection, breaking hexes, spiritual guidance, and blessing the home.

Lavender
Sandalwood
Angelica root

Burn this incense once a week, preferably every Monday morning. You may also burn this incense when communing with your guardian angel.

As You Please Incense

This powerful formula is designed for commanding and compelling works to induce others to go out of their way to please you and do your bidding.

> Cedar
> Myrrh
> Bergamot essential oil

To convince someone of your needs, write their name on parchment paper and place it under the burner. Burn for a few minutes each day until your influence is firmly established. If seeking favor with binding papers or legal documents, pass the documents through the incense smoke.

Attraction Incense

Attraction is a highly magnetic blend which attracts love and entices good spirits. It is a potent love, luck, money, and success drawing formula alleged to conjure love, sex, passion, and luck in relationships.

> Catnip
> Peppermint essential oil
> Cinnamon chips
> Grated orange peel

Burn this incense in your place of business each morning to attract new and returning customers. To attract a love interest, write their name on a piece of brown paper three times, turn the paper 45 degrees, and write your name over theirs 3 times. Then place the paper under the incense burner face up and light the incense.

Banishing Incense

The magickal act of driving away negativity and evil is called banishment. This formula is designed to get rid of illnesses, negative emotions, undesirable people, and conditions. It functions to block negative thoughtforms that may be directed toward you and is excellent for exorcising undesirable spirits, entities, and demons that may be lingering within the home or that may have been sent there to work against you.

> Camphor
> Rosemary
> Frankincense

Burn when you wish to expel an unwelcome visitor from your home. Its strength is increased if the unwanted guest's name has been written on paper, torn into tiny pieces, and mixed into the incense before it is lighted.

Beneficial Dream Incense

This formula is designed to inspire good dreams, promote prophetic dreams, and invite dreams that reveal lucky numbers to give you the edge in games of chance. In addition, it is believed to promote psychic visions and visions that foretell the future. The fragrance is excellent for stimulating the imagination, which in turn makes it a great conjure formula for creative people like musicians, artists, writers, and entrepreneurs.

> Lavender flowers
> Star anise
> Frankincense
> Ylang-ylang essential oil

Burn in the bedroom just before retiring so that the night will draw favorable influences and beneficial spirits who can help to make one's dreams come true.

Better Business Incense

As its name implies, this powerful formula is specifically designed to help a business improve its bottom line.

> Basil
> Cinnamon
> Cloves

Burn daily in your shop and pair with money and prosperity rituals to attract more customers and keep existing customers returning. Pass your business cards through the smoke to imbue them with magnetism.

Bible Incense

This is a special incense for use during Bible study or for smoking your Bible. It can also be burned during altar work, prayer, and meditation, and with protection and blessing spells.

> Frankincense
> Myrrh

Cinnamon chips
Cassia essential oil

Burn this incense near your Bible and pass it through the smoke to more fully understand the scripture under study.

Black Arts Incense
A potent black magick formula, this incense is burned to call upon dark forces and spirits to attack, destroy, and have complete domination over your enemies. Black Arts incense can also be used to summon and control dark spirits for pacts. You should always consider the consequences and ethics of using this formula as it can backfire and attract negative, chaotic energy if your intention is not justified.

Black Pepper
Sulfur
Mullein
Vetiver

To curse someone who has wronged you, write the name of your target on a piece of paper 9 times, turn the paper 45 degrees, and write a power word or phrase on top of and crossing their name 9 times. For example, you can write "I damn you to Hades" or "You will lose everything" over the target's name. Tear up the petition paper in little pieces and burn it with some Black Arts incense while visualizing your desired outcome.

Black Cat Incense
This is a powerful conjure formula that is a favorite among gamblers but also has several other lesser-known properties. For example, it can be used to compel the opposite sex to strongly desire you, and it can be used for breaking bad spells and unhexing.

Sage
Myrrh
Bay leaves

To gain good fortune for yourself, burn each morning upon arising. Bring defeat to another by placing their name, written with Dragon's Blood Ink on parchment paper, beneath the burner and burning at midnight.

Blessing Incense

This incense is a New Orleans Voudou Hoodoo staple for invoking the presence and holiness of the Divine. It is used to bestow blessings, gain protection in troubling times from benevolent spirits, and block enemy attacks.

Lavender
Angelica
Myrrh

Burn this incense to promote a sacred and peaceful atmosphere, create a shield of protection around you, attract positive energy, and draw good fortune to others.

Cast Off Evil Incense

This traditional formula is designed for ridding yourself or your loved ones of negative energy, the evil eye, and evil influences in general.

Rue
Bay
Hyssop
Frankincense

Burn daily to keep jealousy and envy directed toward you away.

Cleo May Incense

Cleo May products originate from an old-time New Orleans formula designed for working girls who sought to attract high-end clientele with the ability to pay large sums of money in return for companionship and sexual favors.

Rose
Vanilla
Orange peels
Myrrh

Before going out on the town, burn this incense to attract men with money, find a sugar daddy, or develop a relationship with someone who has the potential to raise your economic status. Light some Cleo May incense and smoke your sexy parts prior to going on dates to secure a man with means.

Come to Me Incense

Attract a specific person or ideal mate into your life with this formula. It has a sweet and spicy aroma that can create a romantic atmosphere and draw the attention of your lover.

Balsam of Peru
Cinnamon chips
Catnip
Raw granulated sugar

Come to Me incense can be used in various ways, such as burning it on charcoal, sprinkling it on candles, or fixing love letters.

Commanding Incense

Commanding formulas are designed to exert power and control over a person or situation. As incense, it is ideal for domination workings and advancements in work, or other areas in which you want to be in control.

Patchouli
Calamus
Bergamot

To use, write the name of the person or situation you wish to command along with precise statement of the change you seek on a piece of paper. Hold the petition in your right hand tightly and say: *I command you; I compel you (name your target and state what you want them to do)*. Repeat three times, ending with, So be it. Tear the petition up into tiny pieces, mix with the incense, and burn on charcoal.

Crossing Incense

Crossing incense is burned to cause strife, misfortune, and anguish to an enemy. It is often associated with curses, hexes, and revenge spells. Crossing incense can be used to create a hostile environment for someone by burning it in their home or workplace. Like Black Arts incense, it should be used with caution and only for justified reasons, as it can backfire and attract negative energy.

Wormwood
Mullein
Myrrh

To use, burn the incense before a black candle that has been anointed with Crossing oil while visualizing the desired outcome. Write the name of the target on parchment paper and place the petition beneath the candle. In front of the candle, set the incense and light.

Crown of Success Incense
Crown of Success formulas are used in Southern folk traditions when advancement in one's career or education is desired and when success in all worldly affairs is the goal.

> Star anise
> Allspice
> Orange peels
> Amber resin

Burn some of this incense before undertaking exams, certifications, or any specific events related to advancement. Say, "May all my works be crowned with success" as you cense your head and hands.

Domination Incense
Domination incense is effective in all types of domination work. It is traditionally used for gaining power over any person or situation.

> Licorice root
> Lime peels
> Dragon's blood resin

To maintain dominance over all situations and magickally inoculate yourself and your home against curses, burn a bit of this incense in every room of your house each week.

Drive Away Evil Incense
This incense is designed to get rid of evil people, situations, spirits, and forces. It is good used in combination with banishing and exorcism formulas.

> Camphor
> High John the Conqueror root
> Cinnamon

To drive off evil influences, write the biblical passage below and set it under your incense burner. Burn daily until the situation improves.

> Let God arise, let his enemies be scattered, let them also that hate him flee before him.

Easy Life Incense
This formula is used to attract good luck, prosperity, and success, but not in the same way as other luck and success formulas. It is used to influence others to do work for you so you can sit back and enjoy the fruits of their labor.

> Ginger
> Licorice root
> Cloves
> Cassia essential oil

Burn in the presence of those you wish to influence. Write the names of those you need to work for you without complaint on a piece of paper and set it under the incense burner before lighting the incense. Light the incense and focus on your desire.

Egyptian Incense
Egyptian incense is designed to honor the Egyptian deities and to assist the dying. It is formulated to ease the journey in their crossing to a new dimension by bringing pleasant memories into the mind through sense of smell. It can also aid in psychic development and working with the dead.

> Rose
> Myrrh
> Rock rose

Burn in honor of any Egyptian deity. It can also be burned in a sick room or hospice when a person is aware of their imminent passing.

Exorcism Incense
Exorcism incense is formulated to drive out demons, possessions, and hauntings from people, places, and objects.

> Myrrh

Angelica root
Rosemary

A simple exorcism ritual involves burning this incense in every room of the home or space in need of extreme cleansing. Move in a counterclockwise direction. If a person is under the influence of evil spirits, burn some of this incense and have the person pass their hands over the smoke 9 times. Each time they pass their hands through the smoke, say, "You shall not remain with the likeness of my ancestors."

Fiery Wall of Protection Incense

This incense is considered to provide an impenetrable shield from all harm when it is burned daily.

Dragon's blood resin
Cinnamon
Myrrh
Red sandalwood

Accompany the lighting of this incense with the following prayer to St. Michael:

Oh, Glorious St. Michael, Archangel,
I beseech you to fight against those who fight me;
War against those who make war upon me.
Take up the sword and shield and rise up in my defense.
Block the way in the face of my pursuers.
Let those be turned back who plot evil against me.

Has No Hannah Incense

This classic New Orleans formula for good luck is great for folks who have trouble holding on to their money, paying bills on time, or sticking to a budget.

Jasmine flowers
Pine resin or copal
Sandalwood
Gardenia essential oil

Gamblers burn this incense before gambling by smoking their money, wallets, hands, and good luck charms.

Healing Incense

Healing incense attends to the process of healing when burned to create a soothing and relaxing atmosphere. It is believed to have various benefits for the mind, body, and spirit, such as reducing stress, enhancing mood, promoting meditation, and healing wounds.

Sandalwood
Myrrh
Frankincense
Balm of Gilead

Burn daily in the sick person's room to foster healing and encouragement while protecting the rest of the family from harm. While burning the incense, pray Psalm 6:2 or say a heartfelt prayer of your own.

Have mercy on me, Lord, for I am faint; heal me, Lord, for my bones are in agony. My soul is in deep anguish. How long, Lord, how long? Turn, Lord, and deliver me; save me because of your unfailing love.

High Altar Incense

High Altar is an incense burned for uncrossing, healing, and protection. It can also be used to invite the highest order of spirits to your altar.

Lavender flowers
Frankincense
Palo santo

Burn during uncrossing and cleansing rituals. It also has protective qualities making it ideal for burning during healing rituals to protect the practitioner.

Jerusalem Incense

Experience the enduring fragrance of incense used for centuries in churches worldwide since the times of Jesus. Jerusalem incense is used for ritual cleansings. By burning this incense, all impurities are removed, allowing God's blessings to enter.

Cedar
Myrrh
Frankincense

The Marie Laveau Voodoo Grimoire

Cinnamon
Cedarwood essential oil

Compound everything lightly and burn on charcoal. Say Psalm 140 when burning this incense.

Louisiana Van Van Incense
This formula has multiple uses in New Orleans Voudou. It is used for uncrossing, clearing, drawing love, and success. It helps remove negativity, change bad luck to good, uncross crossed conditions, and bring luck in love and business, as well as functioning as a road opener to new opportunities.

Rosemary
Cinnamon
Lemon verbena

Use Louisiana Van Van incense to consecrate and empower amulets and talismans and burn in any space to clear away negativity and open doors to luck and romance.

Obeah Incense
Voudouists use this incense for protection, commanding, and compelling rituals. Obeah may be burned for boon or bane.

Myrrh
Patchouli
Galangal

Burn Obeah incense before other rituals. To empower a candle working, keep some Obeah incense burning constantly until the candle is consumed.

Spiritual Incense
Incense and herbal blends have been used for centuries by medicine people, healers, psychics, and seers to alter consciousness. This is a psychoactive formula, so do not use it if you do not want to experience any psychoactive effects.

Marijuana flowers
Lavender
Frankincense

Burn Spiritual Incense to aid in shamanic journeying, meditation, and inducing dreamlike states. Use enough to get a good smoke going and inhale the fumes.

Temple Incense
Also known as *Ketoret*, this biblical formula was given to Moses by God, who said, "Take fragrant spices—gum resin, onycha, and galbanum—and pure frankincense, all in equal amounts."[41] Biblical scholars differ in opinion as to the identification of onycha. Onycha has for some time been identified as the operculum, the trap door of certain sea snail shells. Given it is not a "fragrant spice" and is procured from one of the unclean animals in the Bible, however, onycha is likely not operculum.[42] A promising contender is labdanum, which is the resin produced by the rock rose bush. The Talmud states that onycha, translated as *shecheleth,* comes from a ground plant or bush called rock rose. Thus, using labdanum as an educated guess, we get the following formula for Temple Incense:

>   Rock rose
>   Frankincense
>   Myrrh
>   Galbanum

Burn this incense during any sacred rite or whenever you are purifying your altar and temple areas. It is an ideal incense to aid in prayer and meditation.

Uncrossing Incense
This extremely potent mixture is used to cast out any hex or enchantment. Burn in every room of the house simultaneously, with all doors and windows closed for optimal results.

>   Frankincense gum
>   Lavender flowers
>   Bay leaves
>   Camphor

Write the crossed person's name on parchment paper and place it beneath the incense burner. Burn this incense and recite Psalm 62 daily for 9 days. On the 9th day, burn the petition paper with the incense. Take the ashes and blow them toward the sunset. Repeat the 9-day ritual monthly until things turn around for the better.

Valentine Incense

This is an old formula for reuniting a couple that has broken up. It can also help to bring two people together. Any perfume can be used, though be sure to use a fireproof dish because the perfume will be highly flammable. It will burn hot and high at first, and then smolder in the sugar. If you don't want to deal with the flames, use rose oil instead of perfume.

Perfume or rose oil
Raw granulated sugar
Red sandalwood

Burn on Valentine's day or anniversaries to set your intention for romance and to celebrate passionate love.

Burning incense is perhaps the oldest custom in the history of humankind. The conversion of gums, woods, and aromatic plants to an ethereal state is believed to be the most effective way to contact and please the spirits. It is an essential practice in Voudou rituals because it helps to attract spirits who can offer advice, healing, or prophecy. Incense also purifies spaces and practitioners of negative energy and creates the necessary mood for ritual activity. Incense was indispensable in Voudou rituals in Marie Laveau's day and remains so today.

Figure 14. Adam and Eve Conjure oil is an attraction formula designed for soulmates and may be used by any gender when the goal is to strengthen the love between two people.

Chapter 8

LOVE MAGICK

One day, Mimmie (Marie Laveau's granddaughter) told me that Marie Laveau got $100 for getting a man for a White woman. I don't know what she did, Mimmie did not tell me that but the people in the neighborhood said that she used to talk to the spirits and use Hoodoo.

—Mrs. Marie Dede, 1939

Among the many modes of enchantment for working on the affections is the love spell. Tales of their marvelous efficacy are a persistent occurrence in historical and legendary lore, and their popularity today remains constant.

In the past it was assumed that making love philtres and casting spells to induce love were among the most powerful of the hoodoo's functions. Invested with this skillful art, they were freely consulted, and reaped substantial monetary profit from believers. But love conjures of the past were designed for a different kind of society, one that did not have cell phones and the internet. The object of your affections would have lived in your neighborhood. You would have practiced old-style conjure, literally throwing powders in someone's path, fixing their doorknobs, and accessing their front porch to plant a gris gris. You would be close enough with a man to rub love oil in the palm of his hand and to collect a sample of semen to use in anointing a nine-knot charm.

Hoodoo is based on the use of roots, herbs, and other natural elements for crafting spells and charms designed to affect the physical and spiritual realms.

One of the most potent ingredients in Hoodoo are bodily fluids, specifically menstrual blood and semen. These fluids are believed to contain a person's essence and life force and can be used to attract, bind, or manipulate a lover. Menstrual blood and semen are often added to food or drinks, or applied to personal items, such as clothing or candles, to influence the target of the spell. In the past, folks were not concerned with the spread of communicable diseases through bodily fluids and so there was no word of caution in deploying such conjures. Today, however, we know that highly infectious diseases can be spread by ingesting an afflicted person's bodily fluids, so keep this in mind when deciding whether or not you wish to engage in such conjure. It is best to get your partner's consent if you want to do so.

An Important Note on the Ethics of Love Magick

Most of the love charms found in the nineteenth and early twentieth centuries are designed for women wanting to get their man, but they are just as easily used by men trying to get a woman or any person wanting the love of another person. That said, I would be remiss not to include a word of caution about love spells. A million workings exist to draw someone to you that you think you really want but who is actually bad for you. They might end up possessive and overbearing, maybe even abusive. Further, a partner gotten through magickal means often requires continual magick to keep them. You should ask yourself if you really want to attract someone who would not normally be your partner. Instead of coercing someone to be your lover, why not focus on the ideal qualities and traits you desire in someone and trust the universe to send that person to you? Just some food for thought. In the meantime, if you have determined that you want to continue to pursue someone using love magick, this chapter has a selection of love conjures stemming from Marie Laveau's day that will have you bewitching in no time.

Note that in these old charms gender was an important distinction in the conjures. In reality, gender is of little consequence when it comes to the principles of sympathetic magick. Feel free to work these conjures as a person of any gender on a person of any gender.

AN APHRODISIAC LOVE PHILTRE

This love philtre has tequila as its base, so if your partner doesn't like tequila or doesn't drink, simply leave it out. Added to the tequila is chai tea, which contains wonderful love-drawing and love-enhancing herbs and spices, including cinnamon bark, cardamom, vanilla bean, and cloves. The antioxidants in chai tea increase blood flow and sensitivity to sexual organs, making it an effective aphrodisiac. Caffeine adds focus and energy. To make two of these alluring love philtres, you need the following:

9 ounces tequila
8 ounces chai tea concentrate
8 ounces blood orange juice
Personal bodily fluids (optional)
Garnish: orange slice and cherry

Shake the ingredients together with ice and strain into two large martini glasses. If you wish, you can add some of your own bodily fluids to the drink. Just be certain you are free of any disease that may spread in this manner before doing so and that you have your partner's consent. Serve the love philtre with an orange slice and cherry speared on an extra-long pick.

TO BIND A LOVER TO A PLACE

This working is from an Obeah doctor named Simeon, who shared it with author Zora Neale Hurston in 1931.[43]

For a woman who wishes to bind a man, she should have him look into a mirror without looking into it herself. The mirror is taken home and smashed to bits. It is then buried under the front steps, and the spot wet with water. This act plants him in place so he cannot leave.

As for a man who wishes to bind a woman, he should cut three locks of her hair. Throw one over his head, hide one in his front pocket, and the other in the back of his watch. Then do the same thing with a mirror as described above. You should be absolutely certain you wish to bind someone because you will be stuck with them, and the work cannot be undone.

TO BREAK UP A COUPLE

This conjure appeals to the spirit of High John the Conqueror by working with the root. For this working, you will need the following:

High John root
Grapefruit
Brown paper
Pie pan
Red pepper
Epsom salts
Sugar
Table salt
5 black birthday or small chime candles

Cut the grapefruit in half. Write the names of the couple you wish to break up on the brown paper and put it inside the grapefruit. Whisper into the High John root what you desire and place it on top of the petition paper inside the grapefruit. Close the grapefruit by putting the two halves back together and placing them in the pie pan. Sprinkle the red pepper, Epsom salts, sugar, and salt around the grapefruit. Set the 5 black candles around the grapefruit in the pan. Light the candles. Pray to Johnny Conker to separate the couple. When the candles burn down, take the grapefruit and everything in the pan and place it under a fruit tree and leave it. Pray again to Johnny Conker to separate the couple. Continue to pray for 9 days, and on the 10th day there should be signs of trouble in paradise.

> To keep a man at home, write his name on a piece of paper, fold it small, and stick it in a jar of honey. Set it where it won't be disturbed and say, "Please be sweet to me." That will keep him well tied.

TO BRING A COUPLE TOGETHER

This is a simple work by Lala Hopkins, a Hoodoo queen in New Orleans during the 1930s and 1940s.[44] Lala was a devotee of Marie Laveau and always gave praise to the Voudou Queen before doing any work to ensure its success.

Lala says to bring a couple together, make a perfume of Vanilla Quick Luck combined with wintergreen and honeysuckle oil. Vanilla Quick Luck is the equivalent to Fast Luck, so the ingredients for this conjure oil would contain vanilla, wintergreen, honeysuckle, and patchouli oils. Anoint a pink candle with the perfume and set it on a fireproof dish. Set 9 lumps of sugar around the candle along with some rose buds. Light the candle. Pour a few drops of the perfume oil into the palms of your hands and rub briskly together while saying, "Man's gotta come, man's gotta come." Lala does not give details about concluding the work, but it is customary to take ritual remains (leftover wax, sugar lumps, and rose buds) and place them in a brown paper bag and leave them at a crossroads. Alternately, you can bury the bag in your front garden or yard.

A CAJUN LOVE POTION

To bring two people together, combine orange flower water, rose water, and 3 small bottles of honey together in a bottle or jar. Add 9 lumps of sugar onto which the couple's initials have been scratched. Pour some of the love potion around the house of the intended lovers if you have access. Then, dip a pink candle into the potion and roll in granulated sugar. Burn the candle on top of the jar for 9 days. Wrap the jar in a red cloth and bury it in a garden.

TO DOMESTICATE A MAN JES LIKE A HOUSE CAT

A Voudou man from the New Orleans' tenth ward was known far and wide for his work in love conjure. He said to keep a man at home, take a strand of his hair along with a dime he has given you and wrap it in a pair of his underwear. Bury the conjure under the front door. This makes him as domesticated as possible—just like a house cat.[45]

TO KEEP A LOVER SWEET ON YOU

"Be sweet on you" is an informal Southern expression used when someone likes another person romantically. To keep a lover sweet on you, write their name on a piece of paper three times and place it in a jar. Add 1 tablespoon cinnamon powder, 2 tablespoons sugar, and enough water to cover the paper. Hide it in a corner of your home, and they will always be sweet on you.

TO KEEP A MARRIED COUPLE TOGETHER

This working is attributed to Madam Smith, a modern exponent of Spiritualism who lived on Annunciation Street in New Orleans in the 1930s. She was known for her séances and love charms for keeping married couples together.

Put a small amount of rainwater into a clean glass. Drop in 3 lumps of sugar and say: "Father, Son, Holy Spirit." Drop in 3 more sugar lumps and say: "Jesus, Mary, Joseph." Then, drop in 3 more lumps while stating your desire. Place the glass in a dark place (never before a mirror), with a clean spoon across the top. The following morning, stir the contents of the glass toward you with the spoon. Then, standing with your back toward the street, throw the water against the house or fence, saying: "Father, Son, Holy Ghost, please grant my favor!"

TO MAKE A LOVER RETURN

Write down the name of the person to return on a sheet of parchment paper. Spray it with perfume. Get a glass of water and set it on top of the paper and slide both under the bed. Get 4 oranges or tangerines and cut them in half. Press the open halves into a bowl of sugar and rub each of the legs of the bed down with the sugared oranges. Do this nine nights in a row and state your intention each time while doing so.

TO OBTAIN A HUSBAND

Old Man George Nelson was a conjure man in New Orleans in 1936. He claimed to be familiar with Marie Laveau's love workings. During several interviews conducted by the Federal Writers' Project, he shared a work for helping those who needed husbands. The person wanting a husband is to take a dime and a piece of stale bread and wrap them in a bit of flannel to form a paket. The paket is taken out over a river, like on a bridge or in a boat, and dropped in the middle of the river. Doing this is believed to change a person's luck, and a good husband will soon be found.

A SIMPLE CHARM TO KEEP A BOYFRIEND

If you believe you are at risk of losing your boyfriend and you are confident he is worth keeping, try this simple charm. Write his name down on a piece of paper and stick it in a jar full of sugar. Cover it well and keep it out of sight of others. This symbolizes containing your lover with sweetness and affection. To keep a girlfriend, get some of her hair and soak it in water for 3 days. Then place the hair in the instep of your shoes and go about your business. This symbolizes closeness and affection but also dominance.

Figure 15. Happy Times, Amor, and Algiers Fast Luck conjure powders for happiness, love, and luck.

Chapter 9

MAGICK DUSTS AND
SACHET POWDERS

*Magic powders are very numerous. One kind when blown against a
door or window, causes it to fly open, no matter how securely it may be
fastened; another, when thrown upon the footprints of an enemy, makes
him mad; a third, used in the same day, neutralizes the evil effects of the
second; and a fourth destroys the sight of all who look upon it.*

—A. B. Ellis, 1965

Sachet powders are one of the oldest forms of fragrance and can be traced
back centuries to when the ancients used fragrant flowers, leaves, and
woods to perfume their bodies and living quarters. Various aromatic
botanicals were ground together, and fixatives were added to the mixtures to
enhance the aroma and lengthen the life of the fragrance. Old-time rootworkers and Spiritualists used sachet powders along with a variety of dirts and conjure dusts in foot track magick to fix petitions and name papers and to dress
candles. Contemporary practitioners continue to use these magick dusts and
powders in the same way.

To make a powder, grind the ingredients by hand using a mortar and
pestle or a coffee grinder to render a fine powder or dust. Then, cut with
rice flour or cornstarch to bulk up the quantity and improve texture. Talcum
powder used to be a popular filler material, but it has since been found to
be toxic. Some folks prefer no filler at all, and that is certainly okay. It really
depends on what kind of powder you are making. Sachet powders are used
in magick spells and can also be worn on the body as they are perfumed.
Using cornstarch as a base for sachet powders gives them a nice, smooth

consistency. Conjure powders and magick dusts are used in spells but may contain ingredients unsuitable for placing on the body. Also, your intention must be considered when determining how a powder is made and used. For example, I wouldn't want to dress myself with Inflammatory Confusion Powder, but I certainly would want to dress a candle for a rival in a debate with such a powder.

Freshly crushed botanicals that are more coarsely ground will retain their fragrance longer than finely ground powders. The higher the ingredients' quality, the more effective the final product. Dirt collected for blending with powders should be cleaned of debris, rocks, and plant material. While unsuitable for use in powders, rocks and debris can be set aside for use in gris gris and mojo bags. After cleaning the dirt, it can be sifted using a hand-held sifter for a nice, smooth consistency. Sifted dirt is easier to blend with other powders.

WAYS TO USE MAGICK DUSTS AND SACHET POWDERS

There are several ways to use powders and dusts ritually. Generally speaking, they may be used by dressing, sprinkling, creating drawings and ritual symbols, wearing on the body, and blowing. This section explains the techniques for using sachet powders and magick dusts in Hoodoo and Conjure.

Dressing items with a powder or dust is often as simple as sprinkling the powder over the item. You can also use a make-up brush or paintbrush to dress items. Gently dip the brush into the powder and lightly dust items with it. Once an item is dusted, shake or blow the excess off. I tap an item and allow the extra powder to fall onto a clean piece of paper, then save it to be used at a later date. Note that when dressing anything, directionality is important. The rule of thumb is to rub or brush downward to remove crossed conditions and negativity (downward-repelling) and rub or brush upwards to draw something to you, such as love or success (upward-drawing).

Sprinkling is a method of directing and dispersing magick dusts and powders by using your fingers, a spoon, or a shaker container to spread the powder over a person, an object, the ground, or the floor.

Powders can be used to create drawings, Voudou vévés, ritual circles, and magick symbols on the altar or floor. Drawing with powder is an acquired skill and requires some practice to get it right, but the results are visually stunning. Take a little powder in your dominant hand and begin at the center of the design going outwards. Use steady and continuous lines without lifting your hand or breaking the powder trail. When the ritual is done, disperse the drawing with your nondominant hand. Wipe the surface with holy water if you have performed a left-handed work.

Wearing powders is as easy as using regular cosmetic powders. You can dress your body with powders simply by dusting yourself with them. They can help absorb moisture, reduce friction on the skin, and prevent chafing, rashes, and odors. To use a sachet powder, wash and dry the area to which you want to apply the powder. Sprinkle a small amount of powder on your hand or a puff applicator and gently pat or rub the powder onto the skin. Avoid inhaling or getting the powder in your eyes, nose, or mouth. Repeat as needed throughout the day.

Finally, blowing is done by placing some powder into the palm or onto a sheet of paper and then blowing it towards a person, place, or direction. To blow a powder, place a large pinch in your upturned palm and gently puff the powder in the desired direction. If blowing on a client, avoid their eyes and nose and avoid using herbs that are irritants.

For the following receipts, grind equal parts of all ingredients in a mortar and pestle or coffee grinder to a fine powder. Any oil should be added after the botanicals are crushed and blended. For a shortcut, purchase the ingredients already in powdered form if available. For sachet powders, add to a base of two parts cornstarch and one part orris root powder. You may also just use the powdered herbs and roots and omit the base powder if you prefer.

ADAM AND EVE POWDER

This powder is used to bring two people together or to strengthen the emotional bond between two people in an existing relationship. It can help draw a couple closer after a fight or conflict as well. Use with red and pink candles.

Balm of Gilead
Dried orange peels
Rose petals
Orris root powder

To use, sprinkle on the body, bed sheets, and the four corners of the home and bedroom.

ANGEL'S DELIGHT POWDER

Angel's Delight Powder is used for blessing the home, attracting love, and invoking the aid of the angels. It is used with white, pink, red, purple, and blue candles.

Angelica root
Frankincense
Myrrh
White sandalwood

For a simple house blessing, sprinkle the floor with this powder. It can also be used for fixing petitions and candles and for adding to mojo bags and gris gris.

ANGER POWDER

Anger Powder is designed to cool down a hot head. If you are prone to angry outbursts and rage, Anger Powder is supposed to help quell the emotions that cause tempers to flare. Use with blue, purple, and white candles.

Lavender flowers
Vanilla bean
Rose geranium essential oil
Angelica root

Sprinkle or blow around a room to overcome feelings of irritation and anger.

AS YOU PLEASE POWDER

As You Please Powder is for commanding and compelling works, and to make others go out of their way to please you and do your bidding. It is said to be good for knocking down walls between two people in a relationship. Use with red and purple candles in works designed to bend someone to your will.

Orange blossom essential oil
Mint
Vetiver
Licorice root
Calamus root

Sprinkle on the ground in front of a loved one, or put some in their shoes, clothes, or belongings and they will be forced to return to you. If this cannot be done, sprinkle where you are sure they will walk. I find the perfect place for this is right by their car door, where they have to step in and out in order to drive somewhere.

COME TO ME POWDER

Come to Me Powder is a very popular powder by today's standards for drawing an ideal lover or desired condition to you. This formula comes from my personal grimoire.

Powdered sugar
Catnip
Myrrh
Magnetic sand

Use to fix bed sheets, feed mojo and gris gris bags, and to dress red and pink candles. This powder may also be used as a floor sprinkle.

CONTROLLING POWDER

This simple recipe can be made at a moment's notice to influence someone to act in your favor. It comes from Raul Canizares's book *The Life and Works of Marie Laveau*. In the section of the book called Marie Laveau's Secret Recipes, he states the formulas come from notebooks Marie wrote "as 'how-to' manuals intended to teach her students the business side of Voudou."[46] Marie Laveau did not know how to read or write though, so unless she dictated to someone else who wrote these things down for her, there could not have been a notebook written by her. That said, Controlling Powder is a popular powder in the world of Hoodoo.

The formula for Controlling Powder is a traditional three-ingredient formula consistent with many old-style conjure receipts.

Cornstarch
Saltpeter
Epsom salts

Sprinkle in the path of your target, in their shoes, or somewhere they will come into contact with it. You may also use it to fix candles and petition papers for use in spellwork.

Easy Life Powder

Easy Life Powder is designed to help create affluence, where making a living is easy, and you are blessed with luck and success with minimal effort. Basically, it is for living the high life without lifting so much as a finger for it. Use with white, green, gold, and yellow candles.

> Orange blossom essential oil
> Mint
> Calamus root
> Cinnamon

Sprinkle this powder in the yard, your home, and your place of business. You may also use it to fix candles and petition papers in spellwork.

Goofer Dust

Goofer Dust is a powder concocted for the express purpose of killing or severely harming someone. Its ingredients vary between practitioners so there is no standard formula, but most contain things like dirt from a graveyard, crushed insects, and other unsavory notions.

> Black pepper
> Graveyard dirt
> Sulfur
> Dried and crushed insects like wasps or scorpions (optional)
> Crushed glass

Goofer Dust can be used in the same manner as any sachet powder. Traditionally, it was largely confined to foot track magic where the goofer was tossed in the path of the target, so they walked over it and thus became "infected" through contact with the feet. Although I am personally not comfortable with prolonged contact with Goofer Dust myself, I have seen references to rubbing Goofer Dust on the hands and then shaking hands with the person being conjured, or merely touching a part of their skin with it so they will come under your spell.

To neutralize the effects of a goofer, sprinkle the found trick with red pepper and salt and throw in a running stream. Covering goofers with red brick dust is another effective neutralizer.

Hell's Devil Powder

Hell's Devil Powder is used for hexing, cursing, and causing extreme pain and strife on an enemy. Use full strength to bring down the wrath of the gods onto your nemesis.

> Crushed ghost peppers
> Cayenne pepper
> Powdered yellow mustard
> Black pepper

Spread in the path of your target or dust their shoes to ensure contact with the feet. You can also use this powder to fix candles and petitions.

Hot Foot Powder

Hot Foot Powder is a traditional powder used in foot track magick to drive off an enemy, make them run in the opposite direction, and give them a condition called "walking foot." The afflicted are not able to walk correctly and sometimes not at all, so their movement is restricted and that in and of itself can keep them away. Often, they will spontaneously walk backward or in a haphazard fashion—to where, nobody knows. Use when you are under verbal, emotional, or physical attack, or have an annoying neighbor, jilted lover, jealous friend, stalker, or abusive partner and you need the offending person to leave the area for good.

> Cayenne pepper
> Sulfur
> Chili powder
> Black pepper

Mix in a base of sifted ant bed dirt. Spread in the path of your target or dust their shoes to ensure contact with the feet. Although online influencers will tell you to fix candles and such with Hot Foot Powder, this is not the traditional way to use it. It is designed for use in foot track magick, not candle spells, because it works on the principle of contagious magick.

Jinx-Removing Powder

Set spiritual boundaries at the doorways and windowsills of your home with this powder to prevent the evil intentions of others from manifesting in your space.

> Rue
> Agrimony
> Red brick dust

Sprinkle around the perimeters of your home and under the doorstep to protect all who live there and prevent the ability of others to cross you.

Lavender Sachet

Lavender is a wonderful herb that is frequently used as an ingredient in Peaceful Home and LGBTQ+ formulas. It has a pleasant fragrance with a calming effect and when combined with musk, vanilla, or vetiver, it awakens the sexy. This formula is for a straightforward lavender sachet powder that you can make to use on its own merit, or as a base for other formulas that call for a heavy dose of lavender.

> Lavender flowers
> Orris root powder
> Cornstarch
> Oil of lavender

Put some of this powder in little cloth bags and toss in your chest of drawers to keep clothing and linens smelling fresh. Place some in a pretty bowl in your living room as Peaceful Home potpourri.

Louisiana Love Powder

Here is an old recipe for Louisiana Love Powder. Use any southern floral bloom for the formula, such as camelia, carnation, gardenia, jasmine, or magnolia. The blossoms are dried, powdered, and blended with a bit of orris root powder.

During Marie Laveau's time, musk referred to the strong-smelling brownish substance secreted by the glands of the musk deer, used and prized for thousands of years as one of the most precious raw materials in perfumery. Because raw musk fetches a hefty price on the black market—at the time of this writing, it is worth more than gold—it has led to the near extinction of the musk deer. Consequently, substitutions for musk—both natural and chemical—are now used. Common natural substitutions include angelica root and ambrette seed. You can always leave it out if you wish.

Orris root powder
Flower blossoms
Musk
Ylang-ylang oil
Bergamot oil

To enchant a lover, procure a letter or other paper with their writing or initials on it. Turn the paper once to the right. Write your petition over the signature. Dress the letter by pouring the powder over the petition, drawing a heart in the powder, then shaking the powder off. Set it under a red candle that has also been dusted with the powder.

Red Brick Dust
Undoubtedly, the most well-known protective conjure dust in New Orleans Hoodoo is red brick dust. It is well-known for its application in pulverized form to the front steps of the home as a means of keeping evil away. You can also use it to nullify an evil work by sprinkling some on top of the crossed object. For protection, add a pinch of red brick dust to candles.

Unsettlement Powder
This formula comes from Lala Hopkins, Hoodoo Queen of New Orleans, and devotee of Marie Laveau back in the 1930s and 1940s.

Filé (powdered sassafras root)
Graveyard dirt
Gunpowder
Flax seed
Cayenne pepper
Salt

Mix the ingredients well. Throw the powder in front of a person's door—whether home, office, or car—to cause them to have a fight and feel perpetually restless and irritable.

Violet Sachet Powder

The scent of violets may remind you of your grandmother if you're old enough, as it was a popular fragrance during the early 1900s. Queen Victoria was said to have favored this delicate, floral aroma, which is perfect for making a luxurious sachet powder. The heart-shaped leaves of the violet have been traditionally used in love spells, and Violet Sachet Powder can be included in any spell seeking to attract love or luck. Additionally, violets are employed in home protection rituals.

Powdered orris root
Rice flour
Violet oil
Bergamot oil
Rose oil

Use to dust petitions, fix candles, add to mojo bags and gris gris, or wear as a dry perfume.

Voodoo Powder

This is a powerful conjure powder that is used as a last resort when your enemy just won't quit.

Myrrh powder
Graveyard dirt
Patchouli
Mullein
Cloves

Use this powder to fix candles, bottle spells, and doll babies. Use before any sort of Voudou ritual to attract the good spirits and appease the negative and restless ones. Sprinkle in the area of the ritual. Sprinkle in all corners, on doors, and on windows, and burn a little with myrrh incense.

After you are finished making the powder, set it inside your gris gris box on your Marie Laveau altar and light a white or blue votive candle and set it on top. Ask Queen Marie to bless the powder for you and tell her what it is for. Leave it on her altar for seven days for full consecration. Pour her a glass of pomegranate wine or sparkling water in gratitude.

Making magick dusts and sachet powders is extremely gratifying for the apothecary-minded conjure worker, granny witch, yarb doctor, and folk magician of any persuasion. It's one of my favorite activities of all when it comes to the art of conjure. A final concern for using magickal powders for workings, however, is to be sure they are concealed so that the work remains secret. If you use a powder that stands out when poured onto a particular surface, you need to take extra pains to hide it. For example, mix the powder with some dirt from the target area so that it blends in with the environment and no one will be the wiser. When you wish to fix a carpet with powder, work it down into the carpet with your fingers. You may have to tint the powder so it blends in with the color of the carpet, so keep this in mind when deploying your work. Follow these tips when working with your magick dusts and sachet powders to ensure success in your ritual endeavors.

THE OLD LAVEAU HOUSE

Figure 16. Rendering of Marie Laveau's house on St. Ann Street
by an unknown illustrator, 1890.

Chapter 10

THE MAGICKAL
HOUSEHOLD

Her house was small but nice. She had servants, a dog, ducks, chickens, plenty of flowers in the yard, and a boy to look after them. She was well-built and could pass for white. Her lips were large and red like the ladies make now with lipstick but hers were just naturally red. She held her head high and walked a straight, proud walk. She walked the street every day and had nice ways for everybody. The steps to her house were red with brick dust to keep away evil spirits and everybody copied her.

—James Santana, 1939

A magickal household implies a happy and harmonious sacred space of your own creation. A magickal home allows you to practice your craft, connect with the spirits, celebrate the seasons, and enjoy the company of your animals, family, and friends. When you infuse your home with positive energy, protection, harmony, and love, you tap into the natural magick that exists in every living thing and every natural process.

In many African-based cultures, women were the primary keepers of the sacred knowledge and rituals that sustained their communities. They were responsible for the domestic sphere, where they performed daily tasks that involved cooking, cleaning, caring for the children, and sometimes working as domestic servants for their white oppressors. These tasks were not mundane or trivial, but imbued with magickal significance and power. Women used their skills and creativity to infuse their homes with protective and healing energies, honor their ancestors, resist and subvert the colonial system, and pass on their wisdom and culture to the next generations. The role of women in the magickal household was vital for the preservation and transmission of their ancestral heritage.

Creating a magickal household does not require a lot of money or time. You can use simple techniques and items you already have on hand or can easily find. In this chapter, I share a variety of tips and tricks for running a smooth household and creating an atmosphere of harmony and love, perfect for maintaining a happy, magickal home.

CULTIVATING HAPPINESS

A happy home begins with a whole mood. Consider the importance of your mindset and attitude. How does food taste when prepared while angry as opposed to when you are happy and relaxed? Does the energy you exude while in a particular state of mind matter to the overall health of your family and household? Does the idea that a "happy mom equals a happy home" hold true? I'll let you decide. For what it's worth, the principles I discuss in this section apply whether you live alone or with a family unit.

Families can be considered organisms of their own; the whole is comprised of the sum total of its parts. The whole family is affected when one part is out of balance or in a funk. When Dad is angry, everyone feels it. It governs how other family members navigate the home. Discord and negativity spread like a contagion. I liken it to a mobile. When you touch one part of the mobile, the whole thing moves. It is impossible to touch a part of a mobile without causing the other elements to move. Only time without touching it allows for calm and balance to return.

I am very conscious of my mindset when cooking and cleaning because I am aware of how my energy and mood affect my family. I often sing while cooking. My energy becomes part of the food I cook when I touch it, clean it, sing over it, and prepare it. I know I am responsible for the nourishment the meal I prepare provides for my family. I want them to enjoy the meal—I want them to smile naturally and say how much they enjoy it. When that happens, I know my work is a success.

We all have a choice regarding the kind of life we wish to lead and the kind of example we want to set for others. Usually, people subscribe to the morals passed down to them by their parents, which are often defined by religion. Marie Laveau was no exception. She lived in service to her community. As a devout Catholic, she lived by the Corporal Works of Mercy. These principles of right living are derived from the teachings of Jesus. They are guidelines for treating people as if they are Christ in disguise. Marie Laveau possessed the quality of self-sacrifice. She would give her last bit of money to a poor person. To every needy person coming to her, a plate of food and a place to rest that day was provided. "Marie Laveau had lots of Indians with her," shared Mary Washington, a seventy-five-year-old Hoodoo queen and card reader in New Orleans in 1940. "She was kind to everybody. People went to her with their troubles and she would feed them." The Works of Mercy are a way to achieve spiritual excellence and a divine depth of character. For Marie Laveau, this was her way of cultivating happiness in the world.

Aside from the Works of Mercy, what was the secret to Marie Laveau's success and happiness? We can glean a few things from her life that we can emulate and apply to our own.

First, she had a strong sense of purpose. Marie Laveau dedicated her life to helping others, whether they were sick, poor, enslaved, incarcerated, or oppressed. She used her Voudou skills to heal, protect, and empower those who requested assistance. She also played an essential role in the social and political affairs of New Orleans, acting as a mediator and a leader among different groups. She was highly regarded and admired by many, while others were intimidated by her absolute confidence.

Secondly, Marie Laveau embraced her Creole identity. She was proud of her mixed-race heritage. She did not let the social atmosphere of racial discrimination and prejudice suppress her ambitions or aspirations. She also celebrated her Voudou faith. She did not hide or deny her beliefs but shared them through public ceremonies and private consultations. She was also a devout Catholic and saw no problems observing the two faiths—especially as she successfully blended them into her own brand of Creole Voudou.

In addition, Marie Laveau must have had a positive attitude to thrive in such trying times. She was known for her charisma, charm, and benevolence, which attracted many admirers and garnered her a large congregation. She did not let her challenges or hardships discourage or defeat her. Instead, she used them as opportunities to excel and succeed.

Finally, it would appear Marie Laveau had a healthy balance between work and play. She worked hard to provide for herself and her family and to serve her community. But she also knew how to have fun and enjoy life. She loved music and dancing, and her ceremonial celebrations on Congo Square, Bayou Saint John, and Lake Pontchartrain are legendary.

Of course, we will never know precisely what Marie Laveau thought or how she felt. Still, we can absolutely admire her achievements and legacy. We can also emulate some of her qualities and habits in our own lives, such as having a strong sense of purpose, embracing our identity, having a positive attitude, and finding a balance between work and play. Maybe then we can find happiness within ourselves.

CULTIVATING JOY

She lived in that house on St. Ann Street because she loved to be herself. That old house meant so much to her. Marie Laveau told me that the spirits told her not to move from the house where she made her money, and she made it there.

—Mary Washington, age 75

Your home should bring you joy. It should be a place of safety, comfort, peace, and happiness, even bliss. Attaining such a sacred environment is entirely possible because you control the who, what, and where of all the energy that enters and lingers there. Marie Laveau loved her home because she made it a safe place where she could be herself. That is a powerful position to be in.

Joy is a divine state of being. It is true happiness that comes from within the soul and is not dependent upon external forces. We were created to be joyful beings; it is our natural state. Sadly, few in modern society can claim to experience a life of pure joy due to powerful societal and personal influences. Though these influences are largely out of our control, we tend to allow them to shape our thoughts, feelings, and behaviors. Many people live through the lens of fear. The choice to do so, whether conscious or unconscious, takes a toll on our mental, emotional, physical, and spiritual health.

All of the above notwithstanding, you cannot control other people. However, you can certainly influence them in positive or negative ways. And for some, there are genuine conditions that cause us to be fearful. I am in no way minimizing those realities. We cannot control the deranged lunatic who decides to shoot up a nightclub because they hate the LGBTQI+ community. We cannot control the Nazis desecrating Jewish gravesites. We cannot control who is responsible for all of the missing and murdered Indigenous women. However, we can vote, hold perpetrators accountable, and find safety in others.

Joy is not out of reach. It is something we should try and attain daily. This can start in various ways, but one way to start is to examine our core belief system and the messages we tell ourselves. Ask yourself, do I deserve to be joyful? If the answer is no, then it's no wonder you haven't been happy.

Here's a trick I taught my patients as a therapist. Write down all of your self-limiting and critical beliefs you hold about yourself on a sheet of paper in one column. On an opposing column, rewrite that belief by changing keywords that limit, suppress, and oppress to positive, liberating, and uplifting words. For example, if your belief is, "I do not deserve to be happy," your rewrite would be, "I deserve happiness." If another belief is, "I can't get a good-paying job because no one will hire me," then your rewrite could be, "I will get a good-paying job because someone will hire me." It is a simple technique that can be done any time you find yourself using words like "can't" and "shouldn't," and any time you tell yourself you are "too fat" or "too skinny," "always fail," and "unworthy." When you find yourself saying these things, you are wiring your brain to reinforce those beliefs with negative experiences. They become a filter for that bias. All of the other experiences in your life that you have had that are positive are relegated to the unconscious mind, and you forget about them. Then what happens is called a self-fulfilling prophecy. What you believe and say about yourself tends to manifest itself. If you constantly tell yourself that you are a failure, then guess what? You will fail. If you tell yourself that you are a winner, then guess what? You start winning. I have helped many people master this technique and find their world changes when they recognize the lies they tell themselves and actively change those core beliefs.

If you struggle with this concept, consider Marie Laveau's life and work. Do you think she could have accomplished all she accomplished as a woman of color in antebellum New Orleans if she was an "I can't" girl? She walked freely around the city, fraternized with white folks, got people out of jail, healed the sick, openly practiced two religions, and made a business out of Hoodoo. Sure, she had challenges, but nothing stopped her from living her life to the fullest.

When your core belief system changes to reflect a positive reality, there is space for joy to grow. It is a slow and sometimes painful process, but it is so worth it. We are all sacred and divine human beings who deserve to experience joyful lives. Open yourself up to the possibility and nurture your soul to create space for joyful living.

St. Hildegard's Cookies of Joy

In this grimoire, I touch on spiritual prescriptions as remedies for various conditions. Spiritual prescriptions include fragrance, rituals, and energies harnessed and created for the express purpose of improving quality of life in a particular area. Creating joy in a home means you must actively surround yourself with that energy. It means not only having a clean space to look at and live in, but also one that smells good and involves eating tasty foods.

Unsurprisingly, one of the things realtors do when staging a home is bake cookies. The smell of freshly baked cookies is divine and taps into a collective unconscious warm and fuzzy feeling that makes a person want to stay in that space. Witches and hoodoos do the same thing and call it magick. Realtors do it and call it a marketing strategy. They use the four elements in making and baking cookies and rely on the environment created along with their skills to close the deal. Sound familiar?

Using our sense of smell to create a desirable atmosphere and mindset is not a new concept, nor is the idea of serving something delicious to butter someone up. Many business deals are made over a good meal—the atmosphere is conducive to manipulation and compromise. Just consider the old adage, "The way to a man's heart is through his stomach." No one understood this characteristic human trait more than St. Hildegard of Bingen, a twelfth-century mystic, nun, healer, and prophet who figured out how to induce joy and happiness through her tasty cookies.

Hildegard lived in a hermitage from the age of eight until adulthood. During that time, she learned to read but never learned to write. She dictated to scribes and developed an alphabet that allowed her to relay messages from God that ran the gamut from spiritual to practical. She gained notoriety because of her vivid dreams and visions that she believed were messages from God. In addition to illustrations of the world as a cosmic egg engulfed in the flames of God's love, her books contained divinely inspired receipts said to cure everything from the common cold to lung disease.

St. Hildegard understood the mind, body, and spirit connection. Over nine hundred years ago, she documented the recipe for her spiced cookies of joy. Her prescription was to eat a cookie at regular intervals to boost feelings of joy and improve positivity. Now that's a prescription I can get behind! Here is her recipe.

1½ sticks (¾ cup) butter
1 cup brown sugar
1/3 cup honey
4 egg yolks
2½ cups all-purpose flour
1 teaspoon salt

1 tablespoon ground cinnamon
1 tablespoon ground nutmeg
1 teaspoon ground cloves

Melt the butter, then cream it with the brown sugar, honey, and egg yolks. Sift the flour and spices together, then add to the creamed butter and sugar mixture. Refrigerate the dough for an hour. Form the dough into small balls. Place on a floured board and press flat. Transfer to cookie sheet. Bake at 350 degrees for 12 to 15 minutes or until the edges are golden brown. Cool for 5 minutes before consuming. Enjoy!

CULTIVATING PEACE

Striving for and maintaining a peaceful home is such a priority among Hoodoo practitioners that there is a whole class of products called Peaceful Home. Peaceful Home is about nurturing loving relationships and maintaining harmony in the home. Using this formula, you can end conflicts so family members are happy and cooperative. According to some, this formula works because it contains basil, considered one of the most important herbs for creating a happy home. It also includes rosemary because it empowers women to be the dominant figure in the house. Specific formulas for cultivating peace in the home follow.

Marie Laveau's Peace Water

This spiritual water is a combination of water from five sources. The sources of water Marie Laveau used can be determined with some degree of accuracy, given the geography and bodies of water in the New Orleans area. The following recipe is an educated guess based on this reasoning. If you do not live in the New Orleans area, I have provided generic water substitutions in parentheses.

Holy water from a Catholic church (holy water)
Water from Bayou St. John (spring water)
Water from Lake Pontchartrain (lake water)
Water from the Mississippi river (river water)
Rainwater (rainwater)

Blend the 5 waters together by the light of a full moon, with no fragrance and no oil.

Peaceful Home Spritz

To create harmony and tranquility in the home, mix orange, rose, and holy water in a spray bottle. Spritz your home with it to create a calm, serene environment that success easily comes to. You can also add some to your regular floor washes and spiritual baths to accomplish the same intention.

Peaceful Home Simmer

Add a High John the Conqueror root, some cinnamon sticks, orange peels, and oak bark to a gallon of spring water. Bring to a boil on the stove. Reduce to a simmer. Allow it to simmer on the stove to drive off evil conditions and bring success home. You can save some of this to add to a spiritual bath as well.

The Rose of Jericho

Figure 17. A Rose of Jericho in its dried form.

If ever there was a peaceful home Hoodoo plant, it would be the Rose of Jericho (*Anastatica hierochuntica*). The Rose of Jericho is a unique plant because of its ability to dry up and repeatedly bloom despite being uprooted from the earth. After the rainy season, the plant dries and drops its leaves, and its branches curl into a tight ball. For all intents and purposes, it dies. However, the plant's fruits remain attached within the ball and can remain dormant for years. When wet again during the rainy season, the ball uncurls, and the fruits open to disperse the seeds. If there is enough water, the seeds can germinate within hours.

The Rose of Jericho has several medicinal uses. If the dried ball is placed in a bowl and allowed to resurrect, women in labor can drink the resulting water to avoid labor pains. It is also drunk by expectant mothers to ensure a healthy baby. Other medicinal uses include treatment for epilepsy, colds, and amenorrhea.

The Rose of Jericho also has a place in biblical lore. It is said to have been the plant Mary clenched in her hands while giving birth to Jesus. Therefore, the plant's blooming is said to be a symbol of the opening and closing of the womb of the Holy Mother.

A Christmas tradition observed by some Catholics involves setting a Rose of Jericho plant in a shallow dish of water so that it blooms at Christmastime. When Christmas is over, decorations are put away and the plant is allowed to dry up. It is then stored with the rest of the Christmas decorations, and the ritual is repeated the following year. A similar tradition is observed at Easter time, only the symbolism parallels the death and resurrection of Jesus Christ.

Not surprisingly, the Rose of Jericho is perceived as magickal and miraculous and has found its place within the Hoodoo tradition. It is believed to bring peace, power, and abundance to the home. To use the Rose of Jericho, place the dried plant ball in a bowl filled with enough water to cover the plant's lower half. Leave it in the water and watch it unfold into a beautiful plant. Do this at nine in the morning or evening on a Tuesday or a Friday while praying the following prayer:

> Divine Rose of Jericho: For the blessings received, the virtues that
> you hold, and the power considered, help me remove the difficulties
> of life. Give me health, strength, happiness, comfort, and peace
> in my home, success in my business, and ability in work to earn
> money to cover the necessities for my home and family. All this I
> ask for the virtues you hold in love to Jesus Christ and his Divine
> Mercy. Amen

Use the water in which the plant rests to bless your home by sprinkling it in the four corners of each room. Sprinkle in the doorway to remove obstacles and allow abundance to enter your home. Use the plant with faith, and you will see miraculous results.

CULTIVATING CLEANLINESS

I love a magical household. When I clean my home, I like to make it an enjoyable experience because whatever energy I am feeling is what I put into my home. I like the feeling I get when I walk into a home that smells of empowering conjure formulas because I know they are working to help create my sacred space. I know that my home environment reflects my inner environment. If there are messes to be cleaned in my home, it is probably a good idea to take a cleansing bath and take care of any emotional baggage that may be getting in the way of an abundant life.

Keeping your home clean is more than just a sanitation issue. It is a spiritual one, as well. Clutter in the physical world creates blockages in the spiritual world, and filth contaminates spaces and repels blessings. You can work all the magick in the world, but if your physical environment differs from your magickal intentions, it will make it much harder for your magick to work. I am not advocating being anal about it and keeping your home spotless; homes are supposed to be lived in, after all. And if you have kids and pets, well, I get it.

Strive for a balance. Clean a space each day or allot ten minutes out of your day to vacuum or wipe off surfaces or organize clutter. Make a game out of it and have your children help you. Reward them by letting them sprinkle grits or birdseed outside the front door afterward to keep evil and negativity away. Or let them set a glass of water on the windowsill to make holy water in the first morning light. Set aside one day a week for deeper cleaning. Even if your home is not spotless—and very few homes are—the act of clearing translates into the world of spirit. That energy manifests itself on all sides of the energetic coin. As long as you are active in your intentions, that activity keeps energy from stagnating and instead keeps it fluid and moving.

To begin spiritually cleansing your home, you should first assess where it needs it. This can save time with cleansing as you will know where the home needs it most and where it needs simple maintenance. An effective way to do this is with ordinary lemons and powdered cloves. Buy a bag of lemons and slice them into quarters. Take the lemon pieces and powdered cloves and hit each corner of each room of the house, including stairwells and hallways. Sprinkle a little of the ground cloves and place a slice of lemon on top, open side up. Leave overnight. After 24 hours, retrieve the lemons and put them in a brown paper bag. Observe the lemon slice before placing it in the bag for any darkness or other visible impressions. If it is clear, then that space is good to go. If it is not, then that indicates that the room needs cleansing. Lemons are used routinely in conjure to cut through stubborn negative vibes, and cloves draw in abundance, prosperity, and harmonious speech. Once the energy is cleared by the lemons, you are left with the positive, fruitful energy of the cloves in your home.

Now that you know where to concentrate your cleansing efforts, you can begin that process. Clear the clutter in that room. Clean the floors with a good floor wash. If you have carpeting, sprinkle some Van Van carpet sprinkle first and allow it to sit for five minutes before vacuuming. Wipe your windows clear with plain vinegar. Wipe your baseboards with Chinese Wash. Smudge the room with sage, or burn some good incense like Temple, sandalwood, or camphor. Finally, light a white votive candle or tealight in the center of the room and allow it to clear any remaining stagnant energy.

Chinese Wash

Chinese Wash is one of my favorite formulas. I keep a bottle of concentrate ready for use and a bottle diluted with water in a spray bottle to wipe down wooden furniture and spot clean. It is also a great all-purpose floor wash. Use it to clear away negative energy, draw luck and clarity, and keep your home and space open to receiving new opportunities. The name comes from the fact that it was originally made with Chinese herbal ingredients, such as lemongrass, citronella, and camphor.

> 8 ounces Murphy oil soap
> 60 drops Louisiana Van Van Oil
> Piece of frankincense or myrrh gum

Pour the Murphy oil soap into a bottle and add Van Van Oil. Drop a piece of frankincense or myrrh gum into the bottle. Shake well. When you are ready to mop, fill your bucket with hot water, add 2 to 4 ounces Chinese Wash, and clean your floors as usual. To make Chinese Wash for use in a spray bottle, dilute the potion with distilled water.

For Clean Windows

For spotless windows, use holy water and ammonia to remove ordinary dirt and grime and stagnant spiritual residue. Alternatively, you can use vinegar in a similar fashion.

To Clean a Fireplace

Before cleaning a fireplace, sprinkle a good handful of damp tea leaves among the ashes. This makes the dust lift easier and prevents it from flying about the room.

Cologne Water

Cologne water is another of those popular potions you could find in late nineteenth-century households. To make some for cleansing and blessing your home, combine a dram each of oil of lavender, oil of rosemary, oil of lemon, and oil of cinnamon into a bottle. Add 2 drams of oil of bergamot. Add a pint of Everclear or vodka and gently shake. Pour into a spray bottle to use as a smudge spray.

Conjure Your Laundry

Conjuring your laundry is an easy Hoodoo hack to achieve and maintain harmony in the home. You can also use this technique to make a chaos agent move out of the house or to increase the sexy quotient between partners. Determine your intention and identify an appropriate conjure oil to help you manifest that intention. You can refer to chapter 11 for a list of conjure oils and how to make them to help you decide. For example, to get children under control, you might use Bend Over Oil, which is a subtly coercive formula. If you are having issues with faithfulness, you could use Black Devil Oil, which is formulated to bring the wanderer under control and compel them to return to a state of fidelity. Once you have decided your intention and have your condition oil ready, simply add it to the liquid laundry detergent, cap it, and shake. At this point, you can state your intention aloud or silently, depending on the level of privacy you have. Then wash as usual.

To keep a long-term conjure going, you can add a 4-dram vial of Peaceful Home or other condition oil into the main laundry detergent container. No one will be the wiser and everyone who uses it will be blessed by wearing their clothes, using towels, and sleeping in sheets that have been charmed with your intention.

Be sure that the oil you use is strained from any botanical matter before adding it to your laundry. You can use a wire mesh or paper coffee filter to strain your oils. Also be sure that the oil is completely blended into the detergent to avoid oil staining.

> Save your lemon and orange peels. Dry them in an oven at 275 degrees or in a dehydrator. Pound in a mortar and pestle, then transfer to a jar and close. Label and place on your apothecary shelf.

Orange and Lemon Water for Cleansing

Cleaning the home with citrus waters has long been practiced because they are great refreshers and degreasers for cleaning countertops and sinks and adding to mop water. They pack a double punch for their magickal properties as well. Orange water attracts money, prosperity, and love, while lemon water is excellent for cutting ties, opening roads, and blockbusting. Each has a positive effect on mental clarity and focus. So, you can't go wrong when using citrus water to clean the home physically or spiritually.

To make orange or lemon water the old-fashioned way, pound the fresh peels in a mortar, then add to a pot and cover with boiling water. Let simmer for about 15 minutes, then allow the water to cool. Transfer the water to a mason jar and close it. Store in the refrigerator. Use it to wipe counters, mop the floor, and add to bathwater for a refreshing bath.

Order in the Spiritual Court

Lawdy, lawdy, Miss Clawdy, if there isn't something practitioners fail to do that seems so obvious to avoid doing, it is keeping their sacred spaces clean and clear of clutter. Why is this such a challenge for so many of us? It is likely due to a combination of reasons. We move way too fast in the world today, leaving less time for tending to things that matter. We lack organizational skills and fail to take the necessary time to tend to our altars and shrines. Some folks don't think it is that important, so they ignore the dust bunnies forming behind the images of the saints sitting on the mantle. For these and many other reasons, we tend to neglect our altars and sacred spaces to the detriment of our spiritual well-being.

It is incumbent upon us to make time to develop good spiritual habits. Our behavior in this area affects not only our own spiritual well-being but also the spirits and deities we serve. Some of them hate filth (here's looking at you, Erzulie Freda) and demand their altars be spotless. If we fail to maintain their altars appropriately, they will be unable to hear our petitions and unwilling to help even if they could. Think about it; these are gods, goddesses, and familial ancestors we work with. Do you really want to invite them to a dirty home and an unclean altar or shrine? And then arrogantly expect them to do you a solid?

Altars are alive. They must be maintained and cleansed, and the spirits that they house and for which they hold sacred space need to be fed. Altars are created from the same elements that make up our physical bodies—earth, water, fire, and air. These four elements are impermanent, meaning they evaporate, fade, and die if not cared for. Flowers wilt and die, water evaporates, candles burn down, food offerings spoil, and incense turns to ashes. Keeping your altar clean and alive is essential to the magickal household.

Note that in Africa and Haiti, you will see altars that, from a contemporary American perspective, appear to be a literal mess. The surfaces are dirty, and remnants of animal sacrifice, including blood, are spilled upon the surfaces and floor. In this case you have to keep in mind cultural differences. Floors are quite often actual dirt floors. They may not have vacuum cleaners, Swiffer mops, and Chinese Wash in a spritz bottle, as we do, and their conception of cleanliness differs from ours. In West and Central Africa, many altars are outside on the ground, and there can be a buildup of offerings on a particular shrine over a period of months or even years. This is not considered filth or neglect. It is actually an accumulation of power over time. Removing and cleaning the blood, palm oil, and other offerings from the shrines would nullify the spirits' power. As we do not practice animal sacrifice in New Orleans Voudou and have different living standards, you should not compare one tradition to another. Our tradition is a New World one that is young in comparison and, over time, has evolved with characteristics and traditions of its own.

HOODOO YOUR BODY CARE PRODUCTS

Fixing your body care products is easy peasy, especially body oils and massage oils. You can just add the desired conjure oil into a body oil, massage oil, or lotion and shake gently and thoroughly. Preparing your body care products is another way to build conjure into your daily life and relationships.

If you are operating on the down-low, you will have to be cognizant of the color of the conjure oil to be mixed with your body product, particularly if the product is in a see-through container. If the oil is thoroughly blended, however, you usually can't tell something has been added unless you haven't strained the herbs from the oil.

Fix Your Liquid Hand Soap

I am a real fan of this conjure hack and I do it daily. It is one of those workings you can do to really integrate Hoodoo into your life as a daily activity. Once your soap is fixed, you just set it and forget it. And every time you wash you are charming your hands to manifest your intention. Don't underestimate the power of simple conjures such as this one.

While I try to avoid quoting scriptures unnecessarily, there is a biblical precedence for being concerned with our hands in the context of handiwork: "For we are God's handiwork, created in Christ Jesus to do good works, which God prepared in advance for us to do."[47] Likewise, there is precedence for concerning ourselves with our hands in Paganism and Witchcraft, as we are to be stewards of the earth, do good works, and leave a positive influence. If you make some of the special handwash and keep it in your bathroom or at your kitchen sink, then each time you use it you will not only receive blessings throughout the day, but you will also be reminded of the fruits of your labor.

First, start with a hand soap that has some resemblance to your desired outcome. For example, if you want prosperity in your home, you can choose a handwash with basil in it. Basil is associated with both a peaceful home as well as abundance and prosperity. Those cheap dollar store varieties are perfect and within everyone's budget. I like to choose the ones scented with magickal herbs like basil (attracts money and prosperity) and lime (extracts negativity and stagnation). Then, add a few drops of a particular conjure oil to the soap. Shake gently, and voilà! You have success at your fingertips.

To incorporate a regular spiritual handwashing into your daily routine, add 13 drops of Peaceful Home Oil into a bottle of lavender vanilla liquid hand soap and use it whenever you wash your hands. Pray to Marie Laveau, "Holy Mother of New Orleans Voudou, hear my prayer. Bless me with the gentle power of Li Grand Zombi, that I may walk in balance, equally male and female. Holy Mother of New Orleans Voudou, pray for me."

Fix Your Pomades

Fixing your pomades is almost as easy as fixing your laundry detergent and hand soap, but it does require an extra step. Because pomades are not liquids and tend to be wax-based, you will have to heat up the pomade in order to blend in the oil. If your pomade is in a glass jar, then you can just heat it up in the container for about 15 to 20 seconds in the microwave. If it is in a metal or other non-microwaveable container, you will have to scoop some out of the container and transfer it into a microwave-safe bowl. After the pomade is liquified, add 5 to 7 drops of your oil into the pomade and stir well. Transfer the fixed pomade back into its container and allow to solidify. Then you can use as desired.

Conjure oils that work well with this technique include King Solomon's Wisdom Oil and Crown of Success because they work directly with your head. These formulas are used to dress the heads of those who are in preparation for an examination or as a blessing for health concerns. Whether dressing oneself or someone else, it is customary to say, "May all your works be crowned with success" when doing so.

Fix Your Shampoo
Fixing your shampoo is another easy conjure hack. As with the liquid hand soap and laundry detergent hacks, all you have to do is decide your intention, choose your conjure oil formula, and add a small amount to your shampoo bottle. I always go by an odd number of drops, usually 13. That way it's not enough to mess up your shampoo formula but plenty to infuse it with the magickal qualities according to the principles of sympathetic magick.

If you are prone to oily hair, you may opt for using essences instead of oils. Essences are made with water and alcohol and won't exacerbate an oily scalp. In addition, not enough of the essence will be added to your shampoo for it to cause excessive drying. Be sure to shake the bottle gently to ensure the oil or essence is distributed throughout the shampoo. I would advise shaking the bottle each time prior to shampooing as sometimes oils separate from the soap.

WARDING THE HOME

Once your home is cleaned, cleansed, and blessed, the next step is to put protections in place. This is referred to as warding the home. Warding the home prevents negativity from manifesting in the first place. See chapter 12 for how to do this.

Chapter 11

CONJURE OILS AND
SPIRITUAL WATERS

*Boil onion peel or garlic. Strain, add steel dust, geranium or verbena
oil, and restrain. Put up in quart bottles. To bring good luck to your
house, mix a bottle of this concoction with half a bucket of water and
use for wiping the sills and steps. Also throw some in the backyard.
Holy water, orange water, and olive oil are also used in the above-
mentioned manner.*

—Lala Hopkins, 1937

The formulas in this chapter are comprised of a product list from the
1938 *New Orleans City Guide,* the 1910 New Orleans Pharmacy
Museum receipt book, Zora Neale Hurston's *Mules and Men,* and
those passed down through oral tradition attributed to Marie Laveau. As the
list provided in the first source does not include formulations, the recipes
are derived from several vintage and contemporary sources, including nineteenth-century pharmaceutical, cosmetic, and perfumery formularies; the tat-
tered little notebook of receipts in the New Orleans Pharmacy Museum; *The
Life and Works of Marie Laveau* by Raul Canizares; and my personal formulary.
As a source of New Orleans Hoodoo and Voudou formulas, the New Orleans
Pharmacy Museum's formula notebook in particular is an invaluable resource
for authentic New Orleans receipts.

Many of the names of the various oils and powders in this book have
survived the test of time and can still be purchased by conjure doctor contem-
poraries. I carry nearly all of them myself on my website, creolemoon.com.
To maintain the authenticity of the formulas, the ingredients in the following

Figure 18. War water can be used as a curse reversal by sending malevolent energy back to its source.

THE MARIE LAVEAU VOODOO GRIMOIRE

formulas reflect the ingredients advertised by chemists, druggists, and shop-keepers during the 1800s in local newspapers. Among the essential oils and other ingredients readily available at that time were bergamot, anise, almond, orange, lavender, cassia, citronella, cloves, peppermint, rose, and bay, as well as coriander seeds, ginger root, and sulfur (referred to as brimstone). The list is in alphabetical order for easy reference.

ALTAR OIL

Altar Oil attracts beneficial spirits to the altar and is used to open and close rit-uals. New Orleans practitioners use Altar Oil along with Holy Spirit and Lou-isiana Van Van—referred to as the Holy Trinity of blessing oils—when doing spells for blessing and consecration. Altar Oil is the perfect all-purpose spiri-tual oil.

Calamus
Myrrh
Cinnamon

Combine the ingredients and cover with olive oil. Over time the fragrance will strengthen. Use to anoint yourself and others, altars, and ritual tools. Use with white candles.

BEND-OVER OIL

Bend-Over Oil is used when you want to dominate, subjugate, and force another to do your bidding. Described as a gentle persuader by some, Bend-Over Oil is designed to make others willing subjects to do your bidding. As such, it is a coercive and commanding recipe but very subtle in how it works. Use it with red and purple candles.

Calamus
Licorice root
Bergamot
Vetiver

Add herbs to a base of almond oil fixed with vitamin E to prevent rancidity. A common practice is to anoint the inside of your target's shoes each day to keep them under your thumb. To get customers to purchase more at your place of business, anoint door handles, bathroom faucets, and any chairs or other seating. You may also anoint a doormat outside of your business, as this is something customers will walk on to come inside. Finally, as a potent, coercive formula, Bend-Over may be used to break jinxes and to send malevolent thought forms and evil spirits back from whence they came.

BERGAMOT OIL

Bergamot and lemon oil were the two signature fragrances in nineteenth-century households. Nearly everything was scented with one or the other or both, from hair pomades to hand creams. Unsurprisingly, Marie Laveau was one of the most famous users of bergamot oil. She used bergamot oil for hair care, as well as for spiritual purposes. One of her followers, Cecil Hunt, reported in 1940 that Marie once sent him to buy bergamot and incense powders from a drugstore. Bergamot oil is believed to have many magical properties, such as attracting money, offering protection, and drawing benevolent spirits. It is used to anoint candles of different colors for different spells: green, yellow, and gold for money; purple and white for protection; and white for good spirits.

BLACK CAT OIL

Black Cat Oil is an oil with multiple uses but tends to be placed into three main categories by modern conjure workers: gambling, love, and hexing. As a lucky gambling oil, Black Cat Oil is traditionally used to give gamblers an edge in games of chance. It is especially useful in high stakes games, as the oil is said to pull all of the luck in the room to the person wearing it. Black Cat Oil is also used to reverse bad luck.

One recipe for Black Cat Oil given in *The Life and Works of Marie Laveau* by Raul Canizares is a hexing oil. Canizares says to start with a can of machine oil, light a black candle, and pray the Our Father backward at midnight. In the morning, it will transmute into Black Cat Oil. Unfortunately, Canizares does not mention the purpose of the oil, but any old-school conjure worker worth their weight in lodestones will recognize the use of motor oil and recitation of prayers in reverse as a hexing ritual.

The formula below comes from my personal formulary for a love, luck, and money-drawing Black Cat Oil. It also has several other lesser-known properties. For example, it can be used to compel the opposite sex to strongly desire you, and it can be used for breaking bad spells and unhexing.

3 black cat hairs
Mint
Cinnamon
Catnip
Pyrite
Almond or golden jojoba base oil

Use to anoint money or wear as a lucky perfume. Use it to anoint white, green, yellow, and gold candles.

BLACK DEVIL OIL

Despite its seemingly dark title, Black Devil Oil controls marital infidelity by harnessing the reigns of an unfaithful partner and compelling them to return. Its method of action is reportedly based on harming the adulterous relationship. Use it with red and purple candles.

Licorice root
Lavender
Rosemary
Sugar

Combine ingredients in grapeseed or almond oil. Use it to fix your target's shoes and underwear or add some to water when washing clothes. A clever and sneaky trick is to pour a few drops into your partner's shampoo or body wash.

DEVIL OIL

Devil Oil is a type of Hoodoo oil that is used to cause harm, confusion, or bad luck to one's enemies. To make this potent hexing oil, combine all ingredients and top with mineral oil. Use it with red, brown, black, and purple candles.

Chili powder
Sulfur
Black mustard seeds
Devil's Shoestring

Some of the ways that Devil Oil can be used include anointing a black candle and burning it while cursing someone who has hurt your family, sprinkling it on someone's doorstep or property to bring misfortune, and adding it to a bottle spell or a doll to afflict someone with illness or pain.

DICE SPECIAL

This oil is for use with games of chance, particularly throwing dice. Use it with green, gold, and yellow candles.

> A pair of tiny dice
> High John the Conqueror root
> Alfalfa
> Clove oil

Combine ingredients in grapeseed or almond oil fixed with vitamin E. Just before playing, apply to the hands and rub briskly together. Anoint lottery tickets in a five-spot pattern and set under a green candle. Recite the Lord's Prayer followed by Psalm 121:1–8.

ESSENCE OF ANGER

Essence of Anger serves the same function as Anger powder in that it is designed to cool down a hot head. Whenever you feel out of control with anger or rage, you can use this essence to calm down and look at things rationally. To make Essence of Anger, you will need the following:

> Lavender flowers
> Vanilla bean
> Angelica root
> Spring or distilled water
> Everclear or apple cider vinegar
> Rose geranium essential oil

As this is an essence and not a conjure oil, the process for making this formula differs from most of the others in this chapter. Combine the lavender, vanilla bean, and angelica root in a bowl and cover with spring or distilled water. Leave the mixture out under the sunlight for 3 to 6 hours. Strain the botanicals from the water and add an equal amount of Everclear or apple cider vinegar as a preservative. Add some of the rose geranium essential oil until it smells like you want it to smell and your essence is complete. Use with white and blue candles.

FAST LUCK OIL

Fast Luck is designed to bring good fortune in money, gambling, love, and things in general. This particular formula was found in the New Orleans Pharmacy Museum's notebook used by the original compounding pharmacists in 1910. It is as authentic as you can get, outside of talking to a rootdoctor from the same era.

Oil of cinnamon
Oil of bergamot
Oil of verbena or lemongrass

The notebook does not give quantities, so you must approach this receipt like any other Hoodoo formula. You can start with equal amounts and then add to a base oil like grapeseed or fractionated coconut oil fixed with vitamin E. Use it with green, yellow, gold, red, and white candles.

FLORIDA WATER

In Hoodoo, Florida Water is used in spiritual cleansings and home protection. It can be worn on the body, used as an ingredient in magical works or by itself as a cologne, put in the bathwater, and misted in the environment to purify it. In fact, there are so many ways Florida Water can be used it is no wonder it remains a favorite spiritual water among practitioners.

3 ounces bergamot oil
1 ounce lemon oil
1 ounce English lavender oil
12 drops clove oil
20 drops cinnamon oil
Tincture of benzoin
1 gallon alcohol
1 pint rose water

Combine all ingredients and shake well before use.

FOLLOW ME BOY

According to oral tradition, this recipe was created by Marie Laveau. Initially designed for prostitutes, this recipe has money, love, and protection herbs incorporated in it. The blend is favored by sex workers, exotic dancers, and others in the adult industry for its power to attract, seduce, and enthrall. Follow Me Boy ensures financial gain and increased profits.

Catnip
Licorice
Jasmine
Rose absolute
Vanilla

Mix everything in a base of sweet almond oil fixed with vitamin E. You can use this oil as a perfume when going out, add to the bath, or use as a massage oil if you dilute it with more sweet almond oil. Use to anoint red, white, pink, and blue candles.

GERANIUM OIL

Marie Laveau is said to have favored geranium oil.[48] She likely used it in her beauty routines and to anoint candles. Geranium oil also has health benefits, and she may have used it in her nursing activities. Geranium oil is widely used in perfumes and cosmetics. It is thought to have antioxidant, antibacterial, anti-inflammatory, antimicrobial, and astringent properties. The essential oil is also used in aromatherapy to treat a number of health conditions. In aromatherapy, essential oils are inhaled using a diffuser or diluted with carrier oils and applied to the skin for soothing benefits.

Marie Laveau would not have been aware of the recent discoveries and benefits of geranium oil, but that doesn't mean she didn't use it medicinally. It can be added to foot washes and used to massage the legs and feet of the infirm—especially for people suffering from edema.

HOLY OIL

Holy Oil is a special formula used for consecrating altars and ritual tools. It consists of 2 parts pure olive oil, 1 part myrrh, and 1 part Balsam of Peru. Use only with white candles.

HOLY SPIRIT OIL

One of the Holy Trinity all-purpose blessing oils in New Orleans Voudou, Holy Spirit Oil is for anointing altars and ritual tools.

Angelica root
Frankincense
Myrrh

Combine the ingredients in a base of olive oil. Use with white candles.

HUMDINGER OIL

Ole John was a rascal. He used to stay dressed up. Marie Laveau did not want John to work. He used to help her with her work. People used to say that John was an old Hoodoo man himself and did his business with the women. He had a way of making the women like him. I heard a person say that John used Johnny Conker and some kind of a love oil that Marie Laveau prepared for him. It sure did work cause John was what you call a "humdinger."

—Marie Dede, 1939

This oil is inspired by the reputed charisma of John Laveau, Marie Laveau's grandson, who had a reputation for putting on the charm for the women who fell for him. He reportedly used High John the Conqueror root and Marie Laveau's special Love oil to gain mastery and influence. Here's the formula:

High John the Conqueror root
Magnolia essential oil
Rose essential oil
Vetiver essential oil

Blend oils in a base of Jojoba oil and add a small High John root. Use with white, red, pink, blue, and purple candles.

KING SOLOMON WISDOM OIL

Use King Solomon Wisdom Oil with spells for increasing wisdom and insight. For added power, do these works during a waxing moon to take advantage of the moon's increase in size.

Cedarwood essential oil
Frankincense essential oil
Solomon Seal root
Cinnamon essential oil

Blend in a base of golden Jojoba oil and add a small piece of Solomon Seal root. Use with white, yellow, green, and purple candles.

LEGBA OIL

Papa Legba is the most important loa in the New Orleans Voudou pantheon because in order to communicate with any of the other spirits, the practitioner must first ask his permission. It is he who holds the locks and keys to the universe and to the gates to the world of the Invisibles. Marie Laveau often called upon Legba through St. Peter, the saint who holds the keys to the gates of heaven. Here is a recipe for a ritual oil for Papa Legba.

Basil
Anise
Ginger
Pinch of honey tobacco

Blend in a base of fractionated coconut oil. Use with red and black candles.

LOUISIANA VAN VAN OIL

Louisiana Van Van Oil is one of the three Holy Trinity all-purpose blessing oils in New Orleans. It is a multipurpose oil used for uncrossing, clearing, drawing love and success, and just about anything else you can think of. The following formula comes from the pages of the New Orleans Pharmacy Museum formulary. Interestingly, the formula does not contain vervain, aka lemon verbena, so I added it.

Oil of cinnamon
Oil of lemongrass
Oil of rosemary
Lemon verbena and/or lemongrass

Add equal amounts of the above essential oils to a base oil, like grapeseed. Adding some loose herbs to the oil is customary, so add a pinch of lemon verbena and/or lemongrass to your bottle. For best results, I highly recommend first decluttering your home—especially if you seem to be facing roadblocks at every turn—then adding some Van Van oil to a floor wash. You can also add a few drops to your bathwater, add some to your hand soap, burn in an oil diffuser, wear it as a perfume oil, add to your laundry to dress your clothes, and anoint white, green, and yellow candles with it.

> The Holy Trinity of all-purpose blessing oils in New Orleans
> Voudou consists of Van Van, Altar, and Holy Spirit oils.

LOVE DROPS

Priced at just twenty-five cents, Love Drops was top of the list of items available to those who inquired at the local New Orleans Hoodoo drugstore in the 1920s. The formula is designed to enhance the bond between two lovers and to bring two lovers closer together.

Honey
Cloves
Cinnamon
Mint

Combine all ingredients in a base of almond oil to which a little vitamin E has been added to prevent rancidity. Use with red, pink, and blue candles.

LUCK AROUND BUSINESS

Here is a recipe for drawing good luck and paying customers to your place of business. It was reportedly used by prostitutes in New Orleans since early times.

Pulverized dollar bill
Magnetic sand
Powdered frankincense
Heliotrope flowers

Combine all ingredients and cover with gold jojoba oil or sunflower oil to which a little vitamin E has been added to prevent rancidity. Use with green, yellow, and gold candles.

MAGNET OIL

Magnet Oil is designed to draw desirable things to your life such as love, a job, and money.

Magnet
Mineral oil
Clove essential oil
Orange essential oil

Place the magnet on a Holy Bible and leave it out overnight under a full moon. Then put the magnet in a bottle and cover it with mineral oil. Add several drops each of orange and clove essential oil for a lovely fragrance.

MARIE LAVEAU CONJURE OIL

Here is a formula you can make for working with the Voudou Queen, Marie Laveau. She is commonly petitioned for healing, employment, love, money, justice, and court cases.

Gardenia
Vetiver
Rose

Combine the ingredients in a base of golden jojoba oil. Place the oil on her altar for a period of seven days while burning a blue seven-day candle dedicated to her. After the seven days are up and the candle is burned down, the oil will be ready to use.

MEXICAN LUCK

This product was listed in the New Orleans City Guide without indicating whether it was an oil, powder, or incense. Further, an authentic Mexican Luck formula could not be located. Therefore, I drew upon my Latin American roots to create a recipe for an oil that reflects Latin American herbal and mineral correspondences for attracting good luck.

Dried aloe vera leaves
Copal
Tobacco
Piedra Iman (lodestone)

Combine all ingredients and cover with olive oil. Use it with green, yellow, and gold candles.

PAPER WASP BANISHING OIL

Here is an old formula designed to drive an undesirable person away from your home or city for good.

9 black peppercorns
Walnut hulls
Pine oil
Paper wasp nest

Add peppercorns and walnut hulls to the pine oil. Place the paper wasp nest in the oil mixture and store. Refill with pine oil when needed. Use to anoint candles, petitions, and doll babies for banishing purposes.

7-11 HOLY OIL

7-11 Holy Oil is another name for the Oil of Abramelin, the holy oil of the Bible. This oil is used for blessings, attracting unlimited abundance, and working miracles. Use with white, green, yellow, and purple candles.

Cassia
Myrrh
Calamus
Cinnamon

Combine the ingredients and cover with pure olive oil. Use to anoint candles, altars, and ritual tools to consecrate and bless them.

SPIRIT OIL

Spirit Oil can be traced back to 1918 in New Orleans, when Mother Leafy Anderson established the Eternal Life Spiritual Church there. Zora Neale Hurston said of the oil, "One can get there a small vial of 'Spirit oil' for fifty cents. The oil is used to anoint one's body against various illnesses and troubles."[49]

Frankincense
Angelica root
Sandalwood
Rose oil

Add the ingredients to a base of olive oil. Add a little vitamin E to prevent rancidity. Pray Psalm 23 over the oil before using it in mediumship sessions, during séances, and any time you wish to communicate with the dead. Use with white and purple candles.

Hurston reports on how to use Spirit Oil according to Mother Hyde, a Spiritualist Mother who "combines conjure and spiritualism." She says to face east and "Read the Twenty-Third Psalm and let that be your prayer. When you come to the part, 'Thou anointest my head with oil,' shake the bottle well and pour three drops on your head and anoint your head. Do this every time you want to conquer and accomplish."[50]

ST. JOSEPH OIL

St. Joseph is the patron saint of New Orleans, and he holds a beloved place in the hearts of Catholics and Voudouists alike. He is considered the patron saint for happy families and those needing employment. Zora Neale Hurston provides a list of ingredients for St. Joseph in her book *Mules and Men* that includes "buds from the garden of Gilead, berries of the fish, wishing beans, juniper berries, Japanese scented lucky beans, large Star Anise."[51] I incorporated some of these ingredients in the following formula that also includes St. Joseph's sacred flower.

Balm of Gilead buds
Fava bean

Juniper berries
Star anise
Lily of the Valley essential oil

Combine all ingredients in a base of olive oil to which a little Vitamin E has been added to prevent rancidity. Use with white candles.

WAR WATER

In Marie Laveau's time, the potion we know today as War Water or Water of Mars was likely not known by either name, though we can't be sure. However, she is likely to have made similar potions and used them in a similar manner as is suggested in modern times. The potion would be placed in a bottle and then tossed against an enemy's front door or side of the house as a threat.

War Water is rusty water containing cut nails, rusty nails, or coffin nails. The nails come from different places to take advantage of their magical correspondences. For example, using nails from a jail would add the element of possible imprisonment for the target. Nails from a hospital would add the element of illness to the conjure. We are working with the law of similarity here, wherein like begets like.

To create War Water, add a little creosote, tar, and Spanish Moss to a base of swamp water in a jar. Toss in a few rusty nails. Allow the potion to sit for a few weeks before use. Wipe it on doorknobs where enemies will touch it or sprinkle it on their doorstep where they will have to walk on it. It is not advisable to throw a bottle against someone's home anymore, as it can be considered domestic terrorism in modern times.

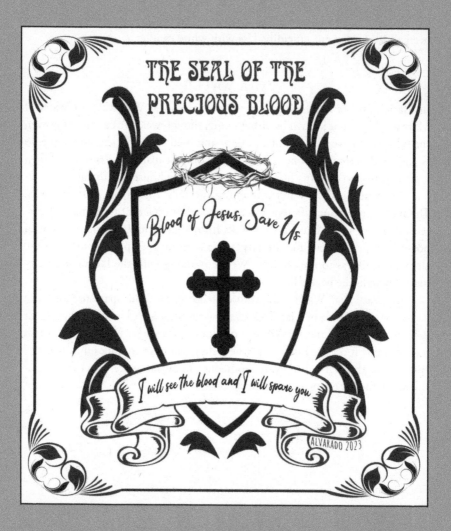

Figure 19. The Seal of the Precious Blood is a protective shield for the home.

Chapter 12

UNCROSSING AND
PROTECTION

*Marie Laveau never let anyone in her house with anything crossed. I
went to her house with a man once and he had two pins in a cross fashion inside his coat. Soon as we walked in the house Marie Laveau told
him, "Uncross these pins before I can do anything for you."*

—Raymond Rivaros, age 64

The belief in the concept of "crossings" is a core psychological com-
ponent of African American folk magic, indigenous spiritual systems, and European-based witchcraft. In each of these traditions,
the effects are the same; but the causal effects are labeled differently. In
African-derived traditions such as Voudou, Hoodoo, and Conjure, for example, to be crossed is to have something bad "put" on you by an external, supernatural force. To be cursed is typically believed to result from witchcraft in
Native American cosmologies. In European witchcraft, to be crossed is to be
hexed. Whatever label is applied to experiencing unfortunate circumstances,
the feeling is the same to the intended target. Just the suggestion of being
crossed is enough to create a self-fulfilling prophecy. In other words, if you
believe things will go wrong, they often will.

In the context of New Orleans Voudou and Hoodoo, the terminology for
crossed conditions is to be *crossed, fixed,* or *jinxed.* A severe streak of bad luck
is likely attributed to someone being jinxed, as opposed to natural life events
or the results of bad choices. The cure is to uncross the affected person, then
traditionally, to put protections in place to prevent further misfortune.

Indeed, feeling you have been crossed does not mean this is the case. In fact, people often cross themselves due to their mindsets and attitudes about the challenges they face in life. Everyone experiences hardship, faces difficult decisions, the death of loved ones, a cut in pay, and an increase in bills—these incidents are not unnatural. They are called life events. What makes one person different from another, and what makes that person seem as if they are "lucky" and "have it easy" is—nine times out of ten—their attitude, how they perceive what lies in front of them and what they choose to do about it.

People regularly sought out Marie Laveau for assistance with removing conjures, reversing bad luck, uncrossing crossed conditions, and gaining protection from experiencing these conditions in the first place. That said, whether you are the source of your own unintended crossing or the supernatural target of an enemy, you can still uncross yourself through ritual action. Performing a symbolic act that represents a desired change often, and quite naturally, results in the desired change.

A BODYGUARD FOR PROTECTION

A bodyguard is a charm created for the purpose of spiritual protection. It is a mojo that is to be carried on the person as a ward against the evil eye and enemies.

Small piece of chamois cloth
High John the Conqueror root
Lodestone
Devil's shoestring
Wishbone
Dragon's blood
7-11 Holy Oil

Place all items on the chamois cloth and add 7 drops of 7-11 Holy Oil to the mix. Sew the chamois cloth closed. Place the chamois packet inside a red flannel mojo bag.

A CHARM FOR PROTECTION

One of the things I love about Hoodoo is its inherent simplicity. There is no need to cast circles and call upon the four quarters to summon a spirit. The charms are often quite simple but no less powerful than any High Magick. Take this charm, for example. Write the names of the twelve Apostles along with Psalm 70 on a piece of paper and pin it on you. The twelve apostles were Jesus's closest followers. Their names were Peter (also known as Simon), James (son of Zebedee), Andrew (Peter's brother), John (James' bother), Phillip, Bartholomew, Thomas, Matthew (the tax collector), James (son of Alphaeus), Jude (Thaddeus), Simon (the zealot), and Judas Iscariot. At each phase of the moon, write them again on another piece of paper and replace the old one for protection.

You can burn the paper to ash each time you change it out. Then you can use the ash to make an amparo on your palm. The amparo is a charm of protection from negative energies and evil entities. Simply take some of the ash, make a cross in each palm, and say one Our Father, three Hail Marys, and one Glory Be.

TO CLEANSE A HOUSE THAT IS CROSSED

Houses, as well as people, can be hoodooed. Using Holy water from a Catholic Church, sprinkle some in the four corners of your home and wash your front door with it. Do this three mornings in a row, and it is said to bring peace and success to your home.

HOLY WATER

Holy water is a commonly used ingredient in Hoodoo, so it makes sense to have some always around. You can mix rainwater with Holy water from a Catholic Church or use it alone. Set a wide-mouthed jar or bowl outside in the rain to catch some water to make Holy water. Only do this at night, and only if there is no thunder or lightning. If it thunders while collecting the rainwater, the water will be contaminated. Bring the water inside before daylight comes. There can be no exposure to thunder or the sun with this method. Immediately say the Lord's prayer nine times with your right hand in the container of water. Then, transfer to smaller bottles and close tightly. Keep your Holy water on your altar for use at a moment's notice for protection against evil spirits and negative energy, and for blessings and purification.

NATURAL MOTH REPELLENT WITH
A SIDE OF PROTECTION

The best grain moth repellent is bay leaves. Sprinkle some in your kitchen pantry, on shelves where you keep food, or even tape some to the inside of food storage containers. Not only will it keep away those pesky grain moths, but it will also bring you protection, health, success, ward off evil and the evil eye, and drive away enemies. Oh, and they won't leave a flavor when stored with your food.

ONE-INGREDIENT UNCROSSING WATER

Boil a High John the Conqueror root in a gallon of water for 15 minutes, scrub your front steps with the hot water, and sprinkle the four corners of your home with it. Do this for nine mornings in a row, and it is said this will break any jinx thrown your way.

> "Many a day I saw Marie Laveau come to the Congo Square. She would walk straight in and not speak to anybody. She came with her black serpent, which she carried in a box. She would put the serpent by the fountain, dance around it a while, then pick it up, put it back in the box and leave without saying a word to anyone. Marie Laveau would do this three or four times a week. People complained about her and two policemen were at each of the four gates at the square. When Marie saw those policemen, she looked at them, never said a word, and walked right in. She just mesmerized those men and a lot of other people, 'cause they never said a word or tried to harm her."
>
> —Breaux, 1939

TO PREVENT LIGHTNING STRIKES

Hang cedar branches around the home to prevent lightning strikes.

RED BRICK FLOOR WASH

To make a wash with red brick dust, add some powdered red brick to a bucket of Chinese Wash. Wash doors and windows to keep out enemies.

REPEL EVIL AND DISEASE

Take an onion and cut it into four equal pieces. Place a piece in each corner of the home to get rid of disease and sickness and keep evil away. Replace the onion when the pieces get black.

RUSTY RAILROAD SPIKES

To ward the home with railroad spikes, plant four rusty railroad spikes in the corners of your lot. If you don't have a yard, place one by your front and back doors to prevent evil from entering the home. You can also put one in a potted plant by the front door. First, wash the spike with soap and scrub it with a steel wool pad. Dry with a clean cloth taking care to notice if any rust remains. If not, coat the spike with a thin coat of Vaseline or mineral oil. Then, anoint them with Fiery Wall of Protection oil and place them in strategic positions.

TO STOP EVIL FROM ENTERING THE HOME

Hang marigolds on your doorpost to stop evil from entering your house.

THE SEAL OF THE PRECIOUS BLOOD

The Seal of the Precious Blood is a protective shield for the home and special items (see figure 19 on page 156). In imitation of the Israelites marking their doors with the blood of the Paschal Lamb to escape the stroke of the Destroying Angel, draw or attach the shield to the back of your front door to prevent illness and misfortune. Attach to objects for similar protection. Then pray to Jesus:

> By the power of the cross and your Precious Blood, please remove from this sacred home all temporal misfortune and keep me free of sin so that I may be worthy someday to sing forever in heaven the praises of the Blood by which we are redeemed.

TO TURN A TRICK BACK ON SOMEONE

If you believe you have been cursed, you can take this three-ingredient spiritual bath to turn whatever negativity sent your way back to its source. Turn your clothes inside out and get three buckets representing the Father, the Son, and the Holy Ghost. Fill them up with warm water and add three ingredients: ammonia (1 capful), saltpeter (just a pinch), and cinnamon (1 teaspoon). Wash with the solution, take the used water and throw it to the east at sunrise. Pray Psalm 36 for protection and to receive blessings from the Divine.

TO UNTIE YOURSELF

To untie yourself, tie nine knots with blue embroidery thread at equal distances from each other in the thread. Anoint each knot with Uncrossing oil. Wear this charm upon your body for nine days. Burn some Temple incense on each of the nine days before a picture of St. Joseph. On the last day, remove the knotted thread and burn it with the Temple incense. Ensure every knot is burned to ash so you will be untied and free again. Blow the ashes outside to the four directions.

TO UNCROSS A HOME

To uncross your home, place a glass of Water of Notre Dame and a piece of High John root in the four corners of your house. Be sure to place them discreetly so they will not be disturbed. Burn some Temple incense every day to drive out the evil spirits and scrub your doorstep or front porch with red brick dust and Essence of Van Van each day at sundown.

Water of Notre Dame can be sprayed about the home to make peace and bring blessings. It can also be used in spells to summon spirits, cleansing spells, and uncrossing works.

Holy water
White rose water
Violet hydrosol
Little John the Conqueror root

Mix the above ingredients and add to a spray bottle. Keep the bottle on your altar or on or near your Bible. Add to uncrossing baths to increase their effects.

Figure 20. Gris gris created by the author for the purpose of power and protection.

Chapter 13

VOUDOU'S CHARMS: GRIS GRIS, MOJO, AND OUANGA

One of the first houses that she had built was on Rampart and St. Ann on the riverside. It was brick. The whole block belonged to her. She was rich. She made her fortune, for it was won in that day by conjuration, gris-gris, and the signs of Moses. She was the mightiest Queen in Louisiana.

—James Santana, 1939

For as long as humans have had the ability for abstract thought, they have attributed mystical powers to simple objects and herbs, transforming the most insignificant plant or stone into a never-failing amulet. The widespread, persistent faith in the supernatural as a means of explaining the inexplicable allows us to organize our experiences in the world in a meaningful way. Laveau Voudou embraces this mystical philosophy with a wide variety of charms, gris gris, mojo, and ouanga.

Charm making is a primary activity of the Voudou conjure doctor. In addition to gris gris, mojos, and ouanga, charms take the form of fixed bones and roots, pakets, tobies, and a whole host of tricks that incorporate powders and curios of all kinds in their creation. They can be made for good fortune or bad and for healing or harming. In the 1800s, "Voudou charms" was the commonly used phrase to describe gris gris, mojo, and ouanga. And while there has always been a tendency to conflate words with each other when it comes to Voudou, the various forms of charms are slightly different from each other.

GRIS GRIS, MOJO, AND OUANGA, EXPLAINED

Gris gris is a complete magickal system originating in Senegambia that was brought to New Orleans with enslaved Senegambians. Senegambians comprised the largest population from Africa to be transplanted to New Orleans during the transatlantic slave trade. Gris gris was a tool of resistance, and employed poisons, charmed waters, bullets, and body gards worn by the enslaved in battles. It served to empower the oppressed, and its use was quite effective. Many enslaved individuals successfully poisoned their masters using gris gris during various insurrections. Gris gris was so effective that it was outlawed, making it illegal to practice.

Mojo, on the other hand, is found in Hoodoo. Mojo bags or hands are small flannel or leather bags filled with a wide variety of animal, mineral, and plant materials, along with seals, metal talismans, and saint medals. Silver dimes, nails, and tar may be added to a bag, depending on its purpose. Mojo bags are considered to be alive when prepared correctly and, as such, must be fed regularly or they will die.

Ouanga, or wanga, refers to Voudou magick. It is also a charm derived from Voudou. It is differentiated from gris gris and mojo in its creation and preparation. Ouangas are typically dedicated to a particular Voudou spirit. They contain things like gunpowder and materia medica sacred to the specific spirit to whom they are dedicated.

Whether gris gris, mojo, or ouanga, the final products are similar. They are often self-contained bags sewn or tied shut. The method of deployment is similar. Gris gris and mojos may be worn on a specific part of the body that corresponds to its purpose. For example, a gris gris may be prescribed to be worn around the waist if created as a fertility charm. It may be prescribed to be worn around the arm if the charm is for strength. And it may be worn at the heart for matters of love and healing relationships or around the thigh in a garter for sex. Ouangas, however, may be kept on an altar, often with a corresponding candle or lamp burning. All three types of charms may also be deployed to a target's front porch or driveway, or otherwise placed in an obvious intimidating place.

In Marie Laveau's day, you could be arrested and sued if you were a conjure worker or Voudouist who sold charms and your charms didn't work. The press made great fun of, quote, unquote, "ignorant superstitious negros." Yet they took it seriously enough to report any arrests of charm makers who found themselves in court due to disgruntled clients. Take the case of one Voudou doctor named William Hastings in 1887 in New Orleans. Mrs. Louise

Tillman, a believer in Voudou, hired Hastings to conjure an enemy of hers. She paid him a total of four dollars and gave him a gold ring and a meerschaum pipe as payment. He reportedly asked for the goods so that he would have some personal items from the target. She wanted her enemy dead. So it was going to cost her. This is actually not contrary to conjure work at all. It can strengthen a working to have personal effects to incorporate into a job, and death conjure is expensive. The press quickly called him a fraud who duped her by asking for the gold ring and smoking pipe to ensure success. Hastings said the gris gris charm was doing the required work. Well, since her enemy didn't die, she pressed charges and Hastings was arrested. After hearing the case, the judge was perturbed by both Voudous. Hastings was fined twenty-five dollars or thirty days as a suspicious character, and Mrs. Tillman ten dollars or twenty days for "trifling with the court." She was severely reprimanded for resorting to such foul means to injure another. Both prisoners were placed in custody.[52]

Another instance involves Marie Laveau herself. While she was often harassed by the police for her Voudou activities and séances, she nonetheless took advantage of the legal system. On May 23, 1871, she filed a complaint against a neighbor, Mrs. Leblanc, for being so full of diablerie as to place a Voudou charm on her doorstep. Front porch conjure was a very common method of putting a fix on someone at that time, and touching the gris gris activates the magick. Laveau's partner removed the charm and got sick, and his illness was blamed on touching the gris gris before it had been neutralized. The judge was not impressed with the belief in Voudou and threw the case out of court.[53]

> Voudou charms and conjure bags are in much demand as talismans against evil. It is considered essential to their efficacy that their possession should be kept secret, the mystery constituting part of the virtue of the charm.

THE GRIS GRIS CAULDRON

The newspapers frequently reported the presence of iron cauldrons and wooden boxes at Voudou ceremonies in the 1800s. "The assembled group assumed an attitude of respect," wrote the *Spirit of Democracy* in 1875. "They made way for their Queen, and a short, Black old woman came upon the scene followed by two assistants, one of whom bore a cauldron and the other a box."[54] Sometimes there are reports of two cauldrons, one for gris gris and the other for gumbo. The wooden box is described as containing a snake; sometimes a snake named Zombi, in reference to Marie Laveau's familiar representing the temple snake. These descriptions were written by presumably white, male nonpractitioners who prefaced their articles with their bias against both Black folks, whom they deemed inferior, and the Voudou religion, which they likened to savagery and cannibalism.

Reading these articles with a discerning eye is necessary to differentiate the propaganda from the facts. As a practitioner of old-school New Orleans Voudou, I believe that cauldrons and wooden boxes were present at Voudou ceremonies in the 1800s. However, the descriptions of what they contained inside them are quite suspect. "Disgust had always kept me from any desire to see this revolting spectacle," writes one correspondent in 1875. That year, he decided to witness a Voudou ceremony for himself and report to the readers "a true description of the barbaric ceremonies practiced by the people whom the military have thrice been used to keep in power over the intelligence and virtue of the community." He's already introduced fifty shades of racism in his opening paragraph, so you can guess where the rest of the article goes with its "true description" of a "barbaric ceremony."

And your guess would more than likely be correct. After a certain amount of "gibberish and wild gesticulation from the Queen," the box was opened, and frogs, lizards, snakes, dog liver, and beef hearts were drawn forth and supposedly thrown into the cauldron. A spectacularly scurrilous scene.

One of the most descriptive accounts of a Voudou cauldron was provided by a reporter in 1870 of Voudou Queen Eliza Nicaux. One of the most powerful queens of the sect at the time—during the decade when Marie Laveau was winding down her public appearances—Eliza presided over the St. John's Eve festival in 1870. It was reported that she had the most elaborate manufactory of charms and amulets on the ground. It was a cauldron mounted on a pedestal draped with black, with a fire underneath, strung about with beads, feathers, and claws of wild animals. Here, with incantations, she prepared powerful charms of beef hearts, bones, and clay.[55]

The charms made from the gris gris cauldron were believed to be most powerful. In Marie Laveau's ceremonies, participants would bring some of their own herbs, roots, and bones to place in the cauldron so that there was a big pot of gris gris gumbo. At the end of the ceremony, during which Li Grand Zombi would no doubt be invoked, each participant was given a portion of the gris gris to take home with them as a potent charm. As some of the participants were adept conjurers, they would use some of that powerful gris gris to create derivative charms for others.

One common narrative around the Voudou cauldron involves participants throwing snakes into the pot. A huge cauldron was put on and filled with water. An older man chanting in Creole added salt to the water. Black pepper was added by a young girl. A box was brought; from it, a black snake was taken and cut into three parts. One of these was put in the pot by the Queen, one by the older man, and the third by the young girl.[56]

I have a few thoughts about this. First, snakes are sacred to Voudou, and killing a snake would be like killing God. In Hoodoo, on the other hand, there was the practice of killing snakes for various reasons, from changing the weather to getting revenge on an enemy. Black snakes were especially used in this manner. This is one difference between Voudou and Hoodoo. Hoodoo without religious taboos is free to engage in such things. In Voudou, the belief in Li Grand Zombi, Damballah Wedo, and Ayeda Wedo precludes one from engaging in that same activity. Moreover, those witnessing the ceremonies often describe themselves as observing from a distance, so how much detail did they actually see? Or is it just a journalistic retelling of a previous article describing something similar, if not verbatim? Truth be told, none of us know what was actually being thrown into those Voudou cauldrons, least of all the typical white male newspaper correspondent in the 1800s.

Another popular story that circulated through the newspapers in the later 1800s was the idea of human sacrifice, especially babies. A number of white babies went missing, and the first to be scapegoated were the Voudous. Who else could be so barbaric as to steal little white babies? "The victim, strange to say, must be white, if attainable, and of such an age as to imply innocent blood."[57] According to a correspondent who claims his information came from a Voudou priestess, there is a version of the St. John's Eve ceremony where a white baby is supposedly sacrificed. An iron cauldron containing a black snake is placed on the ground in the center of the temple. The participants, dressed in loose white clothing, lead a wild, fiendish dance around the cauldron until, one by one, each dancer drops, lying flat on the ground next to the cauldron. After the last dancer falls, the snake is allowed to crawl over each until it touches them all. At this time, the infant is killed, and its blood is sprinkled upon the cauldron, upon the snake, and upon all the worshippers. All this supposedly takes place amid more dancing and wilder, magickal incantations. Ceremonies such as these were of such a secret nature that none but a chosen few were allowed to be present.

Another notorious fable associated with Voudou's cauldron is the black cat sacrifice. According to Robert Tallant, "Sacrifice and the drinking of blood were integral parts of all Voodoo ceremonies. Usually, it was the blood of a kid that was used, but often it was that of a black cat." He even has a chapter in his book *Voodoo in New Orleans* called "Skin a Black Cat with Your Teeth." In Hoodoo and in New Orleans Voudou, black cats are associated with good luck and have been advertised as such since the late 1930s. They are considered particularly auspicious for sports and games of chance. The tail of a black cat when pointing upward was considered lucky, and if you stroke a cat's tail nine times before playing cards, it is said to give you a winning edge. But the most famous of all black cat beliefs is the one that relates to the magic ascribed to the all-powerful black cat bone. Every black cat has one special bone in its body that will either grant the owner invisibility or can be used to bring back a lost lover. Due to these beliefs, black cats were unfortunately sought out for their lucky bones and interred under front porches as well as in the walls of a home for protection, to draw good luck, and to ward off evil.

Cruel rituals such as the black cat bone ritual are no longer condoned, promoted, or practiced by New Orleans Voudouists. In the past fifteen years, I heard of one incident in Louisiana where someone performed the black cat bone ritual. I heard this secondhand and it was reported to my informant secondhand, so the reliability of the report is shaky at best. And while it would make sense that anyone who would perform such a rite would keep quiet about it, word gets around in these circles, and if it were happening with any frequency, rumors would abound.

Gris gris, human, and animal sacrifice are not the only things Voudou cauldrons have been reportedly used for. We also see a strong Congo influence with ancestor pots. I know several New Orleans Voudouists who have ancestor pots. Ancestor pots contain a variety of secret ingredients, including special herbs, sticks, and sometimes human bones, and a skull.

> Marie Laveau knew all the ways of Voudouism, including the charms, the influences, and the rites. In the days of slavery, she made a powerful amount of money selling charms of protection to runaway slaves while they followed the North Star.

MISCELLANEOUS CHARMS

*Their makers are generally old and ill-favored males and females who
have assumed among their race a position somewhat similar to that of
the medicine men among the Indians. They profess to cure many diseases
by means of herbs and oils, but above all it is their province, if properly
paid, to furnish the Voudou which will annihilate anyone near whom
it is placed.*

—Catherine Dillon, 1940

Hair Charm to Steal a Man

Emma Jackson of Algiers shared a hair charm that she contends is guaranteed
to steal a man. Take a lock of hair from the man you desire, a lock of your
own hair, and a dime. Sew it in a little white bag and carry it with you. It is
supposed to make the man crazy for you.[58]

Lucky Bone Charm

The original version of this charm is to use a black cat bone. We no longer use
actual black cat bones due to the cruelty of the rite that must be performed
to procure one; instead, you can use a hollowed-out chicken leg bone, as the
bone needs to be fixed.

Clean your chicken bone well. Make sure it is completely dry. Cut a hole
at the end of the bone and carefully hollow it out. Stuff it with five-finger
grass, lodestone grit, and magnetic sand. Get your lodestone grit by crushing
a piece of a live lodestone; that is, one that is actively magnetic. Pack all of that
into the bone, leaving a little space for some cotton. Work the cotton tightly
into the bone on top of the other ingredients. This will serve as a stopper.
Oil the bone with a lucky conjure oil of your choice. This lucky bone charm
should be carried in your pocket, wallet, or purse. It must be carried with you
at all times and should never be touched by anyone other than you lest it loses
its power.

Money Hand

A mojo hand is also referred to as a mojo bag. It is any odd number of ingredients of animal, botanical, and mineral origin contained in a red flannel or
leather bag. Mojos may also contain manmade tokens or money like silver
dimes, amulets, written petitions, or saint medals.

This Money Hand is for bringing luck in finances and games of chance.
All you need are three things: a St. Peter medal, a St. Raymond medal, and a

silver dime. Place these items into a small red flannel bag. Then, place the red mojo bag into a larger leather buckskin bag. Wrap that bag three times with a thick red thread such as embroidery thread and tie it off with three knots. Turn the bag 45 degrees and wrap it three more times with green thread and tie it off with three knots. Turn it 45 degrees once more and wrap it with yellow thread and tie it off with three knots. Anoint each of the knots with a money-drawing oil and recite Psalm 23 over the bag three times. Feed this Money Hand three times a week by wetting it lightly with whiskey.

Money Paket
Using a piece of newspaper from the stock market section (on a good day) or job-wanted section, cut out a four-by-four square. Add a pinch of cinnamon powder, magnetic sand, 3 cloves, and some basil. Add 3 drops of Van Van oil and 3 drops of cinnamon oil. Fold the paper over the herbs into a little paket and tie closed with string. Tie a coin charm to the paket. Place it in your wallet to keep money coming in.

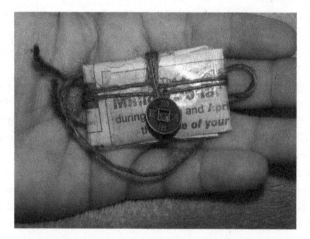

Figure 21. Money paket made by the author to keep money coming in. Photo courtesy of the author.

Onion Skin Charm
Described as a Voudou charm, this formula is unusual in that it marries an incantation with a decidedly Hoodoo activity—burning onion skins. In order to always have money, you should save all of your onion skins and never throw them out. Allow them to dry out and burn like incense in a cast iron skillet, cauldron, or brazier. While burning them, say the Onion Skin Charm:

Honey chile, whenever you use onions fo' ter season,
Don't never trow de skins away, fo' any rhyme or reason,
Jes always burn 'em in de fire—dat part dat you can't use,
An' money sho' will point yer way, to buy you what you choose.[59]

Ouanga for Protection

This ouanga charm is for your personal protection. You need to print out or draw a pentagram or other symbol of power and protection and lay it faceup on your altar. Set down in a triangle formation an incense burner to the bottom right, a bottle of perfume or cologne to the bottom left, and a white candle at the top point of the triangle. The pentagram should be in the middle of the triangle. Lay out a piece of red cloth on top of the pentagram. The size of the cloth will determine the size of the ouanga and how much of each ingredient you will need. If you want to carry the ouanga on your person, use about a 6 -to 8-inch square or smaller. Add some mint, basil, rosemary, sage, frankincense, myrrh, Dragon's Blood resin, some snake sheds, and a small cross. Sprinkle Protection Powder onto the mix. Take a penny and make a wish on it. Place it on top of the other ingredients. Pull the corners of the red cloth together, gathering the herbs into a firm ball, then, using string, tie your ouanga closed like a small bag. If you wish, you can tie a small charm onto your bag that symbolizes protection, such as a sword or an evil eye bead.

Hold your ouanga up and offer it to the four directions: north, south, east, west. Then, hold the ouanga close to your heart and say the following:

Papa Legba, open the gate for me.
May every Mystery guide and protect me.
May Damballah guide and protect me,
May Li Grand Zombi guide and protect me.
Papa Legba, open the roads,
May you guide and protect me, in all paths that I walk.
Ashe! Ashe! Ashe!

Now pray a heartfelt prayer of your own. Sprinkle your ouanga with the perfume or cologne three times. Place it in the middle of the triangle and leave for nine days, each day burning a white candle, replacing the one at the top. At the end of the nine days, you can remove the triangle formation and keep your ouanga on your altar or some other place in your home. Just be sure it is not kept where others can bother it.

Every week your ouanga needs to be fed a white candle and three splashes of perfume or cologne. This should take place at your altar. Each week you can say a prayer over the ouanga. You can also write a petition if you have a special need and place it under your ouanga to keep your intentions and needs current and fresh.

A Prayer to Activate Charms

> God before me,
> God behind me,
> God be with me.
> May this charm bring luck to [person's name for whom the charm
>   is intended],
> May it bind down all devils—bring them under his feet,
> Bring him friends in plenty—bind them to him,
> May it bring him honor, bring him riches,
> May it bring him his heart's desire,
> Success in everything he undertakes,
> May it bring him happiness.
> I call for it in the name of God!

Wishing Charm

Make a little pouch from a piece of black cloth that has been cut round. Add 13 pennies, 9 cotton seeds, and a small bunch of hair from a black dog. Pull up the edges and tie closed with string or leather. Bless the charm using one of the methods described in this chapter. Carry it in your pocket, bra, or purse, and whenever you want to make a wish, take out the bag and rub on it while making your wish.

Chapter 14

SEVEN FOLK RITES OF LAVEAU VOUDOU

Every Monday all the workers and the people who believed in and followed Marie Laveau would come to this tree. They would bring maybe a goat or a chicken or something to drink. Some would bring money—never less nor more than fifteen cents—either three nickels or a dime and a nickel. Everything they did was in threes: one—two—three; Faith—Hope—Charity; the Father, the Son, and the Holy Ghost. These were just the beliefs and practices of her teachings.

—Oscar Felix, 1940

Marie Laveau's Voudou is a folk religion resulting from her intentional blending of Catholicism and Voudou. She openly practiced both religions without conflict and confusion. She could be found praying the rosary in church in the morning, while at night the drums of the Voudous could be heard emanating from Congo Square, where she presided over the celebratory dances of the Grand Zombi.[60] Many of the public rites celebrated today are done in honor of our Voudou Queen.

Although Voudou was firmly in place in New Orleans before the reign of Marie Laveau, it did not have the pronounced Catholic characteristics that we see in New Orleans Voudou during and after her influence. There was already some Catholic influence with the arrival of the Haitians who brought their form of Vodou to New Orleans, but it was Marie's unwavering devotion to the church and integration of some of the sacramentals that firmly fused the two religions together. Doing so was intentional on her part, but why she did it is more complicated than the simultaneous practice of two religions. Voudou

Figure 22. An altar for the Voudou Queen, Marie Laveau.
Photo courtesy of the author.

The Marie Laveau Voodoo Grimoire

was—and still is—illegal in New Orleans.[61] Because of the Louisiana Black Codes, all citizens of Louisiana were forced to convert to Catholicism. And Père Antoine, the Catholic priest who was Marie's dear friend and mentor, was head of the Spanish Inquisition at the time. He did not, however, persecute the Voudous for heresy and instead enabled their practice by allowing them to hold their rituals in the yard behind St. Louis Cathedral so long as Marie brought more people to mass. It could also be that Marie's imposition of the Catholic saints and sacramentals on her congregation offered them some protection. Associating the Voudou spirits with corresponding saints with similar characteristics allowed the worship of the Voudou spirits under the guise of Catholicism.

New Orleans Voudou was and continues to be, for the most part, a matriarchal hierarchical structure. There were kings in the past, but they have always been in the minority and did not traditionally hold the ultimate authority. There are similar practices between Catholicism and Voudou—the burning of incense and candles, veneration of saints, sacramentalism, and charitable work among the imprisoned and the poor. Marie Laveau included Mary in her pantheon, developed prayers and curses, utilized the psalms in conjures, and became famous for her advanced gris gris work.

There are numerous rituals practiced by Voudouists. Every saint and spirit has their own feast day. In addition, major ceremonies are observed, most notably the Feast of St. John, celebrated by congregants since the 1800s. Considered the Holy Days of Voudou, this celebration spans two days, St. John's Eve on June 23, and St. John's Day on June 24. In addition to celebrating the Feast of St. John, these days include celebrating Marie Laveau and Doctor John, the famous gris gris man. I have opted not to include that ceremony in depth here, as I have done so previously in my book, *The Magic of Marie Laveau.*

Individual Voudou houses do not celebrate all of the same feast days or rituals. The rituals observed are determined by the mambo or priestess of the house. Haitian Vodou houses, in particular, will celebrate different feast days according to the spirits observed by that house. They do not observe the same rituals and folk sacramentals observed by New Orleans Voudouists, except for those whose members are from New Orleans. The inclusion of Spiritualist traditions, such as séances, are observed by some New Orleans Voudou houses. All of the tourist voodoo businesses in New Orleans market Hoodoo products as part of their inventory.

Voudou ceremonies are designed to restore order, balance, health, and harmony in the lives of its followers. And in general, Voudou ceremonies are safe spaces for LGBTQ+ individuals. According to *visithaiti.com*, "Cross-dressing, trans identities, and all gender expressions are accepted in Vodou communities. Same-sex relationships are often accepted without question. No one bats an eye—in this space, these minority identities are respected as servants of the goddess of love, Erzulie." Thus, Voudou ceremonies should always be safe spaces.[62]

Because of Marie Laveau, New Orleans Voudou has always had a public face. Visitors have ample opportunity to attend and experience Voudou in a variety of fun and safe ways in New Orleans. Community dances, baptisms, Mardi Gras, St. Joseph's Day, Voodoo Fest, Fèt Guédé, and other lesser-known rituals such as drum circles, hurricane ceremonies, and pouring libations can be observed year-round in the city. Prominent Voudou practitioners such as Cinnamon Black, Priestess Miriam Chamani, Louis Martinie, Sallie Ann Glassman, and the Divine Prince Ty Emmecca grace the city with their public rituals, festivals, educational events, podcasts, and YouTube channels.

There are plenty of private Voudou practitioners as well. For them, rituals are performed at the home altar or outdoors at bodies of water like Lake Pontchartrain, Bayou St. John, or a nearby stream, bayou, or swamp. Rituals are performed in cemeteries, in the woods, or under a special tree in the wilderness or one's backyard.

Some Voudou rites can be replicated and practiced by modern uninitiated practitioners, while others, like the Voudou baptisms, cannot. This chapter introduces seven rituals that can be safely performed by noninitiates interested in developing a meaningful New Orleans Voudou practice. I'd also suggest referring to my book *The Magic of Marie Laveau* for the Vévé and Wishing Tomb rituals and how to become a Marie Laveau devotee. For those who really want to delve deeper into New Orleans Voudou and Marie Laveau, I invite you to explore the courses I offer at crossroadsuniversity.com.

ALL SAINTS' DAY WISHING RITUAL

All Saints' Day is one of the most important celebrations in the Voudou religious calendar. As is the tradition in New Orleans, all Catholic cemeteries host special blessings of the graves on All Saints' Day to encourage prayer and remembrance for the deceased. Special masses are celebrated at all Catholic churches.

All Saints' Day (November 1) and All Souls' Day (November 2) overlap with Voudou's Fèt Guédé, the Festival of the Dead. Like the Day of the

Dead practiced in Mexico and by Latin communities in the United States, Fèt Guédé is an important occasion to honor the ancestors.

Catholics and Voudous visit the cemeteries on All Saints' Day to show respect for the dead by clearing away weeds, whitewashing fences and headstones, and placing floral arrangements on the graves. Before the invention of plastic flowers, women would make *immortelles,* which are wreaths of crepe or waxed paper to sell at churches and cemeteries on All Saints' Day. In less affluent communities, families painted wooden crosses to use as grave markers. Some folks go to the newly cleaned and flower-decorated graveyards at nightfall and place lighted candles on the graves to honor the dead. Voudouists make offerings of candles, flowers, alcohol, and food.

According to Federal Writers' Project informant Mrs. Marie Dede, people never used to put flowers on the tombs of their dead on All Saints' Day. Instead, they would go to the graveyard, clean up around the graves, sit on tombs all day long with pictures of their deceased loved ones, and offer rosaries and prayers for their souls. That was the day Marie Laveau would take a black box and put it on a tomb in the old St. Louis Cemetery and sit on this box all day long until it got dark. Then she would go home. She wouldn't talk to anybody. Some folks wonder why she did this. But when you consider all of her children who never reached adulthood, it is clear to me why she might have spent all day in silence there.

This cemetery rite requires going to three different cemeteries in complete silence on All Saints' Day, so it may be best to go alone. Purchase a clean, white handkerchief or cloth specifically for this ritual. Bless the handkerchief by setting three small white candles in a triangle formation on your altar and placing the handkerchief in the middle of the triangle. Sprinkle a bit of holy water over the handkerchief and pray Psalm 23 three times. Allow the candles to burn all the way down, and your handkerchief is blessed and ready to use.

On the morning of the rite, you must leave home as early and quietly as possible. Not a word or sound must escape your lips from when you close the door behind you until you return. Grab 45¢ in nickels and dimes and stick them in your pocket. Go to the first cemetery and enter the main gate, offer 15¢, knock three times on the gate or the ground, and greet Baron Samedi, who owns the cemetery and everything in it. Without speaking, introduce yourself and tell him why you are there. Although you do not speak, he will hear you. Walk to the opposite side of the cemetery on the main avenue. Somewhere along the way, gather dirt from the walkway and tie it into one corner of the new handkerchief while expressing your most heartfelt wish.

Leave the cemetery by the same gate you entered and go to a second cemetery. Enter this cemetery in the same fashion and pursue the same course, tying a bit of dirt from the main walk into a second corner of the handkerchief with a second wish. Visit a third cemetery and, in the same way, secure a third bit of dirt into a third corner of the blessed handkerchief with a third and final wish. Return home, roll the handkerchief into a compact little ball, and toss it upon the top of an armoire or the cornice of a high window. Any high place likely to be undisturbed and saved by spiders will work.

Then, and only then, can you speak. The charm is broken if a single audible sound escapes from your mouth during this rite. Your wishes will come true before the glow of twelve moons has shed its rays upon you if done correctly.

THE BONFIRES OF ST. JOHN

A major tradition celebrated on June 24 is the creation of the outdoor bonfire in which sacramental items are burned. The fire itself represents the everlasting light of Jesus. These fires used to be huge, communal bonfires, but smaller, family-sized fires are also made. The fire is built at dusk with a blessing from the Roman Ritual and allowed to burn past midnight.

After the blessing, a decade of the rosary is prayed while walking sunwise around the fire. The old sacramentals are reverently burned, and then the party begins. In most places, brave souls leap over the bonfire's flames—an act which is given different meanings in different places. Most say it is an act to bring blessings.

The Bonfires of St. John replaced Midsummer's Eve Pagan celebrations, although people retained some of the Pagan folk practices. People cast pieces of charcoal into the fields for abundant harvests and put ash outside their homes for protection. It is also customary to save some of the ashes from the fire to mix with water to bless the sick.

You can celebrate the Bonfires of St. John in a personal way by adapting the traditional bonfire ritual for individual home devotion. On June 23, gather only things of sacred and sentimental value to burn in a specially prepared fire. You will need a chiminea, cauldron, or another fireproof container.

Sacramental items are any ritual item that has served its purpose. Place all of the sacred items in the fireproof container and light them with a white candle anointed with St. John Oil. While the fire burns, say a prayer to St. John and petition him for blessings of renewal: "Glorious St. John the Baptist, bless this fire and all of the items it will consume." Then, state your petition.

Once everything has burned to ash, sprinkle the ashes with holy water. Keep the ashes to make protection amparos or place them in mojo bags or gris gris for healing. These ashes are perfect for fertilizing St. John's wort plants and your magickal gardens.

> *"Marie Laveau possessed a necklace of glittering beads which she used as charms for lovers. She would display these at the Lay Outs that were given in Congo Square. At these functions, the Queen would sit on a throne-like structure and observe while her followers danced and made merry. During these Lay Outs there was a time set apart for worship. The High Priest would hold a king snake in his hands and the disciples would idolize it by kneeling and bowing in rhythmical sways."*
> —Mrs. Dauphine, 1939

LAYOUTS: SPREADING A FEAST FOR THE SPIRITS

A layout is an arrangement of offerings to a specific spirit or spirits. It has food, liquor, flowers, candles, and herbs on the ground on a white cloth. It can be indoors or outdoors. The color white is associated with the ancestors in African-derived traditions, and in African and Western cultures, white symbolizes purity and cleanliness. Layouts are also referred to as *parterres*.

Layouts typically have candles burning in the four corners of the cloth, with the color of the candles signifying the purpose of the gathering. For example, green is for money, white is for blessings, and red is for love or power. An image of a saint or saints may be placed in the center of the layout. St. Anthony, St. Peter, St. Maroon, and Damballah Wedo were frequently served in this manner in Marie Laveau's day. Liquid libations are placed on the cloth. Alcohol, cider, water, and red drink can be used.[63] Several plates are added to the mix. One contains magnetic sand for drawing something to you; a second contains basil for prosperity and blessings; a third contains cloves for money, luck, and eloquent speech; and a fourth contains cinnamon sticks to quicken the work. Whatever is on the plates should correspond to the purpose of the layout and be favorite offerings of the spirits invoked.

On either side of the layout are two bowls of congris. A small bottle of olive oil is to the left of the saint, and a bag of sugar is to the right. Fresh fruit such as bananas, apples, figs, and pomegranates are added. Herbs are placed in a basket and added to the layout. You may add special stones, bones, and feathers to further adorn the altar and provide additional power to the purpose of the ritual.

To create a layout for Marie Laveau, start by spreading a clean white table-cloth on the ground. On each corner, set a white candle. In the center, set an image of the Voudou Queen and place a blue candle in front of her image. On either side of the blue candle, place a white candle. In front of the blue candle, set a clear glass of water with a crucifix laid across the top. Place bowls of congris and a variety of her favorite offerings such as a mirror, brush, scissors, makeup, Voudou doll, and Mardi Gras beads on the cloth. Lay a single red rose near her photo. Personalize the altar in a manner that speaks to you. Light some incense—it doesn't matter what kind, so long as it smells good and there's lots of it. Place a single palm frond or camphor branch in the front of the layout.

The layout is now ready for your petition, prayer, or meditation. Light your candles and incense, knock three times on the ground, and ask Papa Legba to open the gates.

> Papa Legba, Papa Legba, Papa Legba, open the gates.
> Your children are waiting.
> Open the gates, Papa, and let Marie Laveau through.
> When we are done, we will thank the loa.

Call out Marie Laveau's name three times. Say the Our Father and three Hail Marys, then proceed with your petition. Spend some time quietly meditating and do some divination if you wish. When you are done, thank Marie Laveau for listening to your petition. Ask Papa Legba to close the gates and thank him for his help. You may share the food with anyone participating in the ritual or give it to someone who needs it. After three days, discard her portions of the food by leaving it under a bush or tree outside.

MAKING THE FOUR CORNERS

Graveyard rituals are a popular New Orleans Voudou activity. Marie Laveau engaged in numerous rituals in cemeteries, but one of the most popular of the old-school conjure cemetery rituals is called Making the Four Corners. This ritual is done when special favors are asked of the spirits.

For good luck and to make a special request from the spirits, go to a graveyard. It's best to go to a cemetery with which you are familiar. Ideally, do this ritual on the first Friday or Wednesday of the month. If you can't get there at the beginning of the month, go on a Wednesday or Friday morning. You are going to pray to the Dead at each corner.

Before heading out, arm yourself with a pocketful of nickels and dimes. You will need to knock three times on the cemetery gate before entering. Leave 15¢ in silver coins and a small bottle of rum at the entrance for the cemetery gatekeeper, Baron Samedi. Tell him you have come to make the four corners and are leaving these offerings in gratitude.

Make your way to the northernmost corner, kneel, and place 15¢ on the ground. Say a prayer for the Dead and make your request. Make the sign of the cross. Proceed clockwise to the eastern corner. Repeat as before. Continue to the south and west corners, leaving 15¢, praying, and making your request. When you are done, leave the cemetery and go a different way from which you arrived. This will confuse any meddlesome spirits who may try to follow you home. Once home, it is advisable to take a lavender bath and sleep in white that evening.

MARIE LAVEAU'S BIRTHDAY AND FEAST DAY

Marie Laveau was born September 18, 1801, and her birthday is celebrated with a layout and the burning of copious amounts of incense. If you have the budget, splurge on several bunches of flowers and buy her some perfume. Spritz the perfume all over the altar as you let her know you are offering her these wonderful fragrances and these gorgeous flowers. You can also bake her a cake or offer her French pastries on her birthday.

Marie Laveau died on June 15, 1881, from natural causes. Her feast days, however, are June 23 and 24. When she was alive, she celebrated the eve of the Feast of St. John on this day, but June 23 and 24 are designated days for us to celebrate her life. Make offerings to her of mirrors, brushes, perfumes, and French pastries, and light a blue candle. Creating a layout for her, as described above, is ideal on her feast day or birthday.

THE VOUDOU SÉANCE

I've seen Marie Laveau with these eyes of mine. And that's not all. I sat in on many of her services—what do you call them? Séances! Oh yes, séances.

—William Moore, 1940

My first formal introduction to the world of spirits was at the instruction of my aunt on a Mississippi bayou when I was about five or six years old. There, behind my grandmother's humble little home, she washed my head with an herb bath and taught me how to communicate with the spirits of the Dead with a single white candle. This was my initiation into the mysteries. It wasn't until much later in life that I understood how much of a role séances played in the evolution of New Orleans Voudou and Spiritualism. Though I am not reproducing the precise instructions I received from my aunt here, the following ritual will get you started on a formal method of communicating with the spirits of the Dead.

It may come as a surprise that there is a history of Spiritualist-type activities practiced by New Orleans Voudouists. Is it actually Voudou? Or is it Spiritualism? Well, they are activities that Doctor John Montenée, the Father of New Orleans Voudou, and Marie Laveau, the Mother of New Orleans Voudou, were known for. There is historical documentation for each facilitating these activities. I shared Doctor John's activity as a paranormal researcher in my book *Witch Queens, Voodoo Spirits, and Hoodoo Saints,* and several informants interviewed by the Federal Writers' Project recounted memories of Marie Laveau's séances.

It is important to note that working with spirits is not a game. If you are not careful to observe certain precautions, you may unknowingly call forth entities you may be ill-equipped to handle. Séances open the door to the world of spirits—a door with no filter unless you put one in place. For this reason, some guidelines can be followed to ensure a safe experience when communicating with spirits.

Instructions

It is a popular notion that a séance should consist of three people or any number divisible by three. Although some people will do séances alone, it should never be the case for beginners. My initiation into this ritual consisted of two people, and I successfully performed séances with two people many times afterward. The people you invite to participate in the séance should be believers in the supernatural. They should expect unusual things to happen and not be disruptive due to fear when it does.

First, you'll want to choose a medium. This is a person with psychic abilities, experience with séances, and the ability to traverse dimensions. In New Orleans Voudou, it is a Voudou queen, Hoodoo priestess, or Spiritualist who assumes this role. An experienced medium ensures safety measures before beginning a séance.

Next, decide on a clearly defined purpose. Common reasons for séances include contact with a deceased relative or spirits for divination, guidance, or comfort. The medium states the purpose aloud before beginning and allows anyone present to ask questions and receive answers about the ritual.

Once you've stated your purpose, choose a table. Some suggest a round or oval table. However, I once retrieved an old square table from the top of a bonfire because, according to its owner, it was haunted. She swore by its spiritual activity. While it scared her enough to want to burn it, I had to have it. I have since used it with excellent results. I should also note that the table used at my first séance as a child was a long rectangle one. If for some reason you prefer not to use a table or you do not have one available, you can always sit on the ground in a circle. Items can then be placed in the center of the circle.

Personalize the table to make the ceremony inviting to the spirits. Set a bowl of water, a candle, incense, and other items to create an atmosphere conducive to spirit communication. Minerals like quartz crystals attract spirits, but metals like iron and steel will repel them. Setting a large quartz crystal in the middle of the table can act as a spirit conductor and assist in making contact. If inviting a deceased relative or ancestor, place their photograph or personal item on the table. Be sure to mention that you have set the items there for them.

Light a white candle. Some say to light no less than three candles; however, as I mentioned at the beginning of this section, I was taught to use a single white candle, and it has proved to be effective for fifty-eight years now. That said, if you want to use three candles, go for it.

To get the spirits to visit, remove all light sources from the room except your candle. Close the blinds and cover the windows. Some do not go to this extreme, but as I have learned through participation in very specific Native American ceremonies, any amount of light present can deter the spirits from accepting your invitation to visit. Be sure to remove all distractions and extraneous sources of noise or visual stimuli at this time as well. Turn off TVs, computers, and cell phones unless you are trying to capture paranormal phenomena. Way back in the day, we did not use tape recorders or other devices now utilized in the paranormal research community. However, if you are so inclined, record the session with a tape recorder and refer to it afterward. There may be some audible evidence on the recording device that you don't hear during the ceremony that may be significant.

If you are a practicing New Orleans Voudouist, at this point you would ask Papa Legba to open the door to the spirit world:

Papa Legba, Papa Legba, Papa Legba, open the door.
Your children are waiting.
Open the door, Papa Legba, and let the spirits through.
We ask that only safe and benevolent spirits are allowed passage.
We ask for your protection from spirits who would do us harm.

Note that you should have some offerings on the table for Papa Legba. Some things he enjoys are candy, small toys, a cup of black coffee, three pennies, and a shot of coconut rum. Offerings to him are done in triplicate, except for his drinks. Point these out to him and thank him for his assistance.

Begin to communicate with the spirit you decided to contact. First, introduce yourself. Then, say something like, "We welcome any good spirits who are near us to join our circle. Please make your presence known." If attempting to contact the Voudou Queen, address her by name: "We are reaching out to Marie Laveau. Please join us when you are ready. We have prepared the table with some offerings for your enjoyment."

Facilitate effective communication by indicating a particular type of response from the spirit, such as two knocks for yes and one for no. If a spirit chooses to speak through the medium, ask questions. Many people subscribe to the practice of holding hands throughout the ceremony. However, I have conducted many séances where this was not the case, and it did not affect the results. Whatever happens, it is crucial to stay calm and in control. If things get out of control, end the séance by blowing out the candles, turning on the lights, and telling Legba to close the portal.

When you are done communicating with the spirits, thank them for joining you. Tell them to go in peace. Then ask Papa Legba to close the door:

We thank you for your assistance tonight, Papa Legba. Please close the door now.

State aloud, "The portal is now closed." *Do not forget this step.* It is the most common reason people experience hauntings, possessions, and emotional problems following séances. End the ritual by extinguishing the candles and turning on the lights.

Contact with the spirits may occur in various ways, depending on the ceremony's success. Sometimes, direct contact occurs during the séance and may be perceived through one or more senses. The sense of smell is the most emotive of all and is the most common form of contact. Smelling cigarette smoke when no one is smoking, or the scent of a familiar or unfamiliar cologne are common examples. Another common form of contact is through touch, such as feeling something very cold, feeling something brush up against you, or the slight presence of a hand on the shoulder. Sometimes a spirit may be heard through a sound or a voice. The rarest form of contact is visual. When this occurs, an orb, light, or apparition may appear. In the Native way, little blue lights always signify the presence of spirits; when this happens, sage should be burned, and prayers should be said for them. Also, it is not uncommon for a ghost to appear in a dream of someone who sleeps in the house that night.

A spirit can be present though we may not be aware of it. One good way to measure the presence of a spirit is through a dog's reaction. Dogs are particularly sensitive to the presence of ghosts and spirits. My Italian greyhound Zephyr always barked and talked in his funny Zephyr voice when spirit activity was present. Another sign to look out for is the color of the candle flame. When it burns blue, it is believed to signify the presence of a spirit.

Special conditions can help make spirit contact. For example, strong emotions such as anger, sorrow, and terror tend to attract spirits. Care should be taken to have filters in place if relying on strong "negative" emotions to prevent attracting the wrong kinds of spirits. People, especially women and children sensitive to the world of spirits, often help open the door to the other side. Hypersensitivity also makes them more vulnerable to spiritual attacks. As a general rule, it is not a good idea to have young children involved in séances.

Rain, particularly when there is lightning, helps to make contact. Water, in general, is good for spirit contact, so setting a bowl of water on the table can act as a spirit conduit.

Nighttime is the best time to hold a séance. Many people prefer to conduct séances during what are believed to be peak paranormal hours for making contact. Between midnight and 4:00 a.m., or precisely at 3:00 a.m., are ideal hours for spirit contact. If the goal is to contact a specific ancestor or spirit, the timing of the séance can be crucial. To increase chances of making contact, schedule the ceremony on the individual's birthday, the date of their death, or some other date of significance to them, such as an anniversary or their child's birthday.

Séances can be powerful experiences and are safe when the proper measures are observed. The Dead are not playthings, and séances are not for entertainment only. They are a serious spiritual activity that, when correctly performed, can provide guidance and comfort for those who participate in them.

THE WISHING STUMP

Enter, if you dare, into the New Orleans Historic Voodoo Museum, where an alligator head and a broom hang over the door, placed there for protection from evil. There's a statue of Changó, the orisha of victory, courage, and physical strength. Beneath it is the Wishing Stump, a preserved tree trunk carved with moaning faces. The stump was supposedly used by Marie Laveau and her devotees as a space for making wishes on Bayou St. John. Acquired by the New Orleans Historic Voodoo Museum at some point, it is now on display in the Altar Room. People place old coins, trinkets, and beads on the stump while making their wishes. On the altar is a pocket holding slips of paper where you can write a petition.

In *The Magic of Marie Laveau*, I mentioned a bit of lore about Marie Laveau's Wishing Spot. It was located on the lakeside of Bayou St. John at the intersection of DeSaix Boulevard. There was a hollow tree trunk that functioned like a wishing well where people tossed coins and dollar bills and burned candles in the hopes their wishes would be answered.[64] According to Gloria Jones, who was interviewed by the Federal Writers' Project in 1940, the Marie Laveau Wishing Spot was a stump in the ground that hundreds of people visited on Fridays at noon, three o'clock in the afternoon, and midnight. She reported that sometimes people would visit the spot during the week but most went on Fridays. They would kneel around the stump, make their wishes, and pray. At any given time, as many as five to ten rows of people would be surrounding the stump. They sang Creole Voudou songs and danced, too.

Mrs. Jones, who got the information about Marie Laveau from her grandmother Emelda Mohr, said that the people would show up, rain or shine. A ritual was performed there, but she didn't remember what it was called. She said there was money to be made by Marie Laveau's people, but there wasn't a charge. Any money that was made was from donations. Apparently, they would salute the Wishing Spot "like the Germans do Hitler." As many white people visited the Wishing Spot as did Black folks.[65]

If you visit the New Orleans Historic Voodoo Museum, you can make your wish at Marie Laveau's Wishing Stump there. Write down your desire on a small piece of paper, wrap it around a dollar bill, and drop it into the Wishing Stump. Visualize your desire and knock nine times on the stump. Then offer a prayer to Marie Laveau. Be sure to thank the spirits with a heartfelt prayer and offering when your wish comes true!

If you want to replicate a wishing stump as a focusing tool for manifesting wishes, you can use any stump that calls out "special" to you. If you do not have access to the outdoors where you can find a stump that you can visit regularly, then you can purchase one.

The stump itself functions as an altar. Baptize it and name it. If you can find one with some branches where you can hang offerings, that would be ideal. If you can find one that has a hole or is hollowed out, so much the better. Otherwise, you will need to carve out a hole to place your wishes.

When you are ready to use it, write your petition on a piece of paper and stick it in the stump. Light a candle and some incense to accompany the ritual. Visualize your desire and knock nine times on the stump. Ask Marie Laveau to grant your wish and thank her for her intercession. In gratitude, offer her flowers, a French pastry or Hubig's Pie, and a glass of water.

Figure 23. The author and her conjure dawg Zephyr at
the cemetery crossroads doing the Lord's work.

Chapter 15

SAGE ADVICE AND MARVELOUS SECRETS

Besides knowing the secret healing qualities of the various herbs which grew in abundance in the woods and fields, she was endowed with more than a usual share of common sense, and her advice was ofttimes really valuable and her penetration remarkable.

—*The Worthington Advance*, 1881

BASIC BRAIDED WICKS

To make a basic, braided wick for use in an oil lamp, you will need 3 strips of heavy cotton yarn or string cut to the desired length of your wick. Mix 2 tablespoons of salt with 1 tablespoon of boric acid in a cup of water and soak your cotton yarn in this mixture for at least 12 hours. After the cotton has soaked, lay it on a flat surface outside to dry in the sun. Finally, braid the strips of cotton together to create your oil lamp wick.

CATHOLIC VOUDOU POWER-UP

A power-up to any type of candle working that marries Catholicism and conjure is to light a candle in a Catholic church at the same time you are setting a light for a client. Anyone can light a candle in a Catholic church, so don't be shy should the need arise. The flame will represent you and your prayerful intention long after you leave.

CONJURE BUSINESS ADVICE

If you are a conjure worker, don't be so quick to share your secrets. Everyone's making how-to videos for everything—whether or not they are accurate is another issue—but if you give away all your secrets, it makes you weak as a practitioner and everyone else will no longer need you. Even as I share and teach so much, there are some things that I will never share publicly. The source of my power is for me to know and use; I cannot become an empty vessel by telling all of the mysteries I am privy to from years of devotion and practice.

Marie Laveau agreed with this stance. As Mrs. Mary Washington tells it, she rescued Marie Laveau from a terrible storm where she was lost for three days in 1869. It happened during her St. John's Eve celebration. On this occasion, Marie Laveau was dancing on a box. Others were in skiffs and on barrels. The sky was a silver blue that night and the moon shone brightly. Mary says she wasn't at the dance herself, but her uncle was. She went to the lake three days after the ceremony at exactly 10:30 in the morning. While there, she noticed a woman lying on a box in one of the creeks. She approached the woman and lifted her up, noticing she was wearing a brown dress and a blue veil. She brought her home and gave her a drink of coffee. "You is a good child and I certainly love you," the woman said to Mary in French. Fearing the woman was going to faint, Mary started to go for a doctor but the woman would not allow her. Instead, she rubbed the woman down with a healing oil she had on hand. After a while, the woman began feeling better. "I wish I had known you sooner," the woman said. Wondering who she was, Mary asked her name, and she replied, "Marie Laveau."

Well, of course after that incident, Mary and Marie became friendly. "She taught me lots," said Mary, "but told me not to tell anyone about my business cause other people would use my stuff."[66] One need only be a modern practitioner with a moderate following on social media to experience fake profiles and the rampant theft of intellectual property to know how true this really is. Some things never change, they just acclimate to new environments.

COW TONGUE RITE FOR A REDUCED SENTENCE

The Cow Tongue Spell or Beef Tongue Rite is an infamous Hoodoo ritual traced back to the 1800s in New Orleans. I do not know the exact origin of working with tongues in Hoodoo; it is likely a relic of West African fetish practices. But Mrs. Josephine Jones, who was a neighbor of Marie Laveau as a child, recalls a beef tongue work Marie did to help a man already sentenced to life in prison get a reduced sentence. According to Mrs. Jones, Marie told the man to first ask for a new trial, which he did. She then took a fresh tongue and slit it open. Typically, the tongue is cut lengthwise. Next, she placed the jurors', judge's, and lawyers' names written on paper into the tongue and tied the tongue closed with black thread. After that, she stuck pins and needles all over the tongue. The tongue was placed in a container and then into the freezer. When the new trial came up, the jurors, lawyers, nor judge could say anything bad about the man. The judge said all he could give the man was three months in the parish prison.[67]

Hoodoo Priestess Lala Hopkins provides another version of this ritual.[68] For her big court cases, she would get a beef tongue, split it longwise, and insert the names of the judge and witnesses into it. Then, she sewed the tongue closed with black thread and put it on ice to freeze their tongues. She burned candles so the witnesses became tongue-tied and couldn't speak. After that, she rolled wine apples on the floor so the judge would discharge the case and allow the defendant to roll right out of jail.

DON'T SHARE YOUR STUFF

I am talking about your ritual items. They are not to be shared. If you let someone use something, you must cleanse it and leave no trace of you on it. Of course, practitioners typically do not want to share their ritual tools for a variety of good reasons. One reason is the belief that if another person touches something in your ritual arsenal, then that object becomes contaminated with that person's energy. Another person's energy can mess up your mojo. And there is always the chance that the conjure can inadvertently affect the person touching it. This is why we do not allow people to see or touch gris gris bags or other conjure workings.

JOE LANDRY'S SECRET

Joe Landry lived at 1509 St. Anne Street in New Orleans in 1939. He was interviewed by the Federal Writers' Project about his knowledge of Marie Laveau and her practice. During the interview, Joe shared the following:

> And now I'm going to tell you a secret. See this cup? I drink out of
> it. Then I always turn it down like this so that it will drain and not
> a drop of water is left. And that's what I want to tell you about—

never leave even a drop when you drink coffee or water or wine or anything—that's a way they hoodoo you now. They is still a lot of hoodoos, but people don't know about it and they practice it this way. They carry with them some stuff and they drop it where you left. That's what they want, to work with where your breath has been and then they put a spell on you. It's true, but you mustn't write it down or tell it. It's a secret and they'd get me and you too if they knowed.[69]

MARIE LAVEAU'S AMAZING SECRET CURSE REMOVAL

According to Mrs. Harper, who obtained the information from her godmother, Mary Louise Butler, a Black woman who lived at Avery Island, Louisiana, knew some things about Marie Laveau. The Butler woman said Marie Laveau walked into a certain spot in Bayou St. John and was drowned on St. John's Eve. Among the followers of Voudou and others, there is a superstition that if one walks into Bayou St. John, at this spot, on St. John's Eve, until the water is over one's head, any spell that has been cast on them will be washed away completely.[70]

MARIE LAVEAU'S MARVELOUS CANDLE SECRET

According to Mary Washington, who knew Marie Laveau when she was a child, Marie said to never burn a candle in Church because it gives your luck to someone else. She said what happens is that you light a candle and pray for what you want. Then someone else comes along and lights the candle and prays for what they want. That takes away your luck when they relight the candle. I'm not so sure how often that happens, as the candles we light in a Catholic church are votives and it is not customary to light a candle and then snuff it out. Nor is it customary to pray over someone else's candle. They are allowed to burn down. However, sometimes candles do go out before the candle is done burning. The next person who comes along may relight the candle, and their thoughts and intentions are now primary to that candle. To avoid that scenario, always light all candles at home, where you are sure of the chain of command with regards to your prayers and intentions.[71]

MARIE LAVEAU ROAD-OPENING MONEY CHARM

If you need money, make a delicious custard for Marie Laveau as an offering and take it to Congo Square in New Orleans. This is a historic place where enslaved Africans and free people of color gathered to practice their culture and religion.

To invoke Marie Laveau's assistance, you will need some custard and a small shovel. Dig a hole in the square and pour the custard into it, saying: "Marie Laveau, this is for you, for money—to get plenty of money. Open the door in necessity." Then cover the hole with dirt and leave the rest of the custard as an offering. Thank her for her help and walk away without looking back. You should see an increase in your income soon. Milk may be used in place of custard if need be.[72]

PRIMING A NEW LAMP WICK

To be sure your oil lamp wick burns properly, it is wise to prime it before use. There are a couple of ways to do this. One way is to soak them in hot, melted wax until they are completely saturated and begin to release air bubbles. Once the wicks are saturated in wax, remove them and dip them in water to cool the wax. Lay the wicks flat on a piece of paper and blot away any excess moisture with a piece of paper towel. The wicks should be hard and dry in less than a minute.

Another way to prepare a new lamp wick is to soak it in vinegar. It is said that doing this prevents smell and smoke, and a much brighter light will be given from the lamp.

THE ROLE OF THE TRICKSTER IN CREOLE LIFE

Beware the man with the silver tongue. You know he's a smooth criminal. He'll promise you the world and then some, and he'll say all that you want to hear. Yet he says nothing at all. So divine this paradigm of walking on the edge of the looking glass.

SENDING A SPIRIT BACK TO ITS GRAVE

If for some reason you have inadvertently called forth a spirit by accidentally muttering its name, you can send it back before it wreaks havoc. To do so, you must grab a handful of graveyard dirt from the graveyard you suspect the spirit came from and throw it to the four directions while saying: "Ashes to ashes, dust to dust, from earth you were created, return there you must."

"SHUT THAT GODDAMNED DOOR!"

"There was a woman," said Mathilda Mendoza, "she could hurt you and do you good, but more hurt than good. She could make you sick or die. Her name was Marie Laveau. I never seen her but my husband say she a little yaller woman, real pretty. All the men like her."

Mathilda went on to express how she worried about her husband being hoodooed by Marie. "She could do it, too. She used to do lots of things to people, she had some of the best people in the city mixed up in her Hoodoo. The police for years tried to stop her and her dances, and she'd look at them side-eyed and yell, Shut that goddamned door!"[73]

And thus, my beloveds, we have come full circle.

NOTES

1. All mentions of Marie Laveau in this book refer to Marie Catherine Laveau, born in New Orleans a free woman of color in 1801, and died in 1881.

2. I use the spelling "Voudou" throughout the manuscript to maintain consistency with the majority of the nineteenth- and twentieth-century sources used in my research. It is also used to differentiate it from Haitian Vodou, African Vodun, and tourist voodoo.

3. At the time, there was no differentiation made between Voudou and Hoodoo. The practices and service to the spirits were not separate as they are today.

4. Doug MacCash, "Marie Laveau's Husband Disappeared 200 Years Ago, But an LSU Student Thinks She Finally Found Him," NOLA.com, May 22, 2021, *www.nola.com*.

5. Denise Alvarado, *The Magic of Marie Laveau: Embracing the Spiritual Legacy of the Voodoo Queen of New Orleans* (Newburyport, MA: Weiser Books, 2020), 45–46.

6. Alvarado, *The Magic of Marie Laveau*, 45–46.

7. George Eaton Simpson, "The Belief System of Haitian Vodun," *American Anthropologist* 47, no. 1 (1945): 39, *https://doi.org/10.1525/aa.1945.47.1.02a00030*.

8. The Federal Writers' Project (FWP) was a federal government project created to provide jobs for out-of-work writers during the Great Depression. Catherine Dillon's unpublished Voodoo manuscript is a much-coveted piece of work by researchers interested in New Orleans Voudou and its people. In essence, it is a compilation of interviews, newspaper articles, and other information that Dillon collected over the time she worked with the FWP. Voodoo, 1937–1941, edited by Catherine Dillon. Unpublished manuscript. Louisiana Writers' Project (LWP), Federal Writers' Collection. Watson Memorial Library, Cammie G. Henry Research Center, Northwestern State University, Natchitoches, Louisiana.

9. Alvarado, *The Magic of Marie Laveau, 101–187.*

10. Informant from Algiers, Louisiana, in Harry Middleton Hyatt, *Hoodoo—Conjuration—Witchcraft—Rootwork,* vol. 1. (Hannibal, MO: Alma Egan Hyatt Foundation, 1970), 795.

11. W. W. Newell, "Reports of Voodoo Worship in Hayti and Louisiana," *Journal of American Folklore* 2, no. 4 (January–March 1889): 43, *https:// doi.org/10.2307/533700.*

12. The term used in reference to herbal poisons or harmful gris gris made out of toxic botanicals.

13. M. Pitkanen, *The Experiments of Masaru Emoto with Emotional Imprinting of Water* (June 2018), doi: 10.13140/RG.2.2.24273.07524.

14. "Masaru Emoto—The Healing Power of Water," Lean Mean Fighting Machine, October 16, 2009, YouTube video, 3:15, *youtube.com*

15. "Black Hair: Tips for Everyday Care," American Academy of Dermatology Association, June 15, 2023, *www.aad.org.*

16. See my book *Hoodoo Almanac* 2012 and the article "Seals of the Angels" (pp. 218–222) for the angelic associations and influences on the planets described from grimoire traditions.

17. Cierra Chenier, "The Tignon Law: How Black Women Formed Decor Out of Oppression," NOIR 'N NOLA, March 25, 2019, *www.noirnnola.com.*

18. Alexander Augustine was referred to as Blind Alexander because he was blinded after being beaten with brass knuckles one night on the way home after work. FWP "Marie Laveau." FWP025.

19. *The Lafayette Adviser* [Lafayette, Louisiana], February 18, 1899, page 4.

20. John C. Gunn, *Gunn's Domestic Medicine, Or, Poor Man's Friend, in the Hours of Affliction, Pain, and Sickness* (New York: Charles M. Saxton, 1847), 40–41, *archive.org*.

21. Jeff Grognet, "Catnip: Its Uses and Effects, Past and Present," *Canadian Veterinary Journal* 31, no. 6 (June 1990): 455–456.

22. Rani Anita and Mohan Chander, "Pharmacological and Phytochemical Evaluation of *Calendula officinalis* Linn. For Anti-Anxiety Activity," *International Journal of Pharmacognosy and Phytochemical Research* 9, no. 1 (2017): 119–122.

23. V. Visuthikosol, B. Chowchuen, Y. Sukwanarat, S. Sriurairatana, and V. Boonpucknavig, "Effect of Aloe Vera Gel to Healing of Burn Wound a Clinical and Histologic Study," *Journal of the Medical Association of Thailand* 78, no. 8 (August 1995): 403–409.

24. M. Wijesinghe, M. Weatherall, K. Perrin, and R. Beasley, "Honey in the Treatment of Burns: A Systematic Review and Meta-analysis of Its Efficacy." *New Zealand Medical Journal* 122, no. 1295 (May 2009): 47–60.

25. Preethi K. Chandran and Ramadasan Kuttan, "Effect of *Calendula officinalis* Flower Extract on Acute Phase Proteins, Antioxidant Defense Mechanism and Granuloma Formation During Thermal Burns," *Journal of Clinical Biochemistry and Nutrition* 43, no. 2 (September 2008): 58–64, *https://doi.org/10.3164/jcbn.2008043*.

26. Gardner D. Hiscox, ed., *Henley's Twentieth Century Formulas, Recipes and Processes* (New York: Norman W. Henley Publishing Company, 1914), *gutenberg.org*.

27. C. Ray Brassieur, "Herbal Healing Traditions of South Louisiana," February 25, 2014, page 22, *botanical.pbrc.edu*.

28. Brassieur, "Herbal Healing Traditions of South Louisiana," 27.

29. Mary Harris Frazer, *Kentucky Receipt Book* (Louisville, KY: Press of the Bradly & Gilbert Company, 2022): 358–359.

30. "SAGE: Overview, Uses, Side Effects, Precautions, Interactions, Dosing and Reviews," *www.webmd.com*.

31. Interview with Old Man George Nelson. Federal Writers' Project. "Voodoo, 1937–1941." Folder 25.

32. Brassieur, "Herbal Healing Traditions of South Louisiana," 29.

33. Samuel Owusu et al., "Factors Associated with the Use of Complementary and Alternative Therapies Among Patients with Hypertension and Type 2 Diabetes Mellitus in Western Jamaica: A Cross-Sectional Study," *BMC Complementary Medicine and Therapies* 20, no. 314 (2020); Letizia Polito et al., "Plants Producing Ribosome-Inactivating Proteins in Traditional Medicine," *Molecules* 21, no. 11 (November 18, 2016): 1560.

34. Brassieur, "Herbal Healing Traditions of South Louisiana," 13.

35. R. Morgan Griffin, "An Overview of Black Cohosh," WebMD, December 10, 2022, *www.webmd.com*.

36. Mark Jackson, "'Divine Stramonium': The Rise and Fall of Smoking for Asthma," *Medical History* 54, no. 2 (April 2010): 171–194, *https://doi.org/10.1017/s0025727300000235*.

37. E. Merton Coulter, *Confederate Receipt Book: A Compilation of over One Hundred Receipts, Adapted to the Times* (Richmond, VA: West & Johnson, 1863), 21.

38. Paul B. Hamel and Mary Ulmer Chiltoskey, *Cherokee Plants and Their Uses: A 400 Year History* (Sylva, NC: Herald Publishing Co., 2002), 41.

39. Lowell John Bean, Katherine Siva Saubel, and Harry W. Lawton, *Temalpakh (from the Earth): Cahuilla Indian Knowledge and Usage of Plants* (Banning, CA: Malki Museum Press, 1972), 60.

40. To five-spot a petition paper is to anoint the four corners and the center of the paper with a conjure oil.

41. Exodus 30:34 New International Version.

42. Leviticus 11:9 and 11:12.

43. Zora Neale Hurston, "Hoodoo in America," *Journal of American Folklore* 44, no. 174 (October–December 1931): 317–417, *https://doi.org/10.2307/535394*.

44. Interview with Lala Hopkins. Federal Writers' Project, "Voodoo, 1937–1941," Folder 025:95.

45. Federal Writers' Project, "Voodoo, 1937–1941," Folder 118C:55–56.

46. Raul Canizares, *The Life and Works of Marie Laveau: Gris-gris, Cleansings, Charms, Hexes* (Old Bethpage, NY: Original Publications), 37.

47. Ephesians 2:8–2:10.

48. Interview with Mary Washington, Federal Writers' Project, "Voodoo, 1937–1941," folder 025:127.

49. Hurston, "Hoodoo in America," 319.

50. Hurston, "Hoodoo in America," 320.

51. Hurston, "Hoodoo in America," 278.

52. "The Gri Gri," *The Times-Picayune* (New Orleans), July 7, 1887, 8.

53. "Bad Charms," *New Orleans Republican,* May 24, 1871, 5.

54. "Negro Incantations at New Orleans on St. John's Eve," *The Spirit of Democracy, Woodsfield, Ohio,* July 27, 1875, 1.

55. "Voudouism," *Northumberland County Democrat,* Sunbury, Pennsylvania, August 5, 1870.

56. "The Voudou Festival," *New York Times,* July 7, 1872.

57. "Voudouism," *The Charleston Daily News,* July 15, 1870, 1.

58. Federal Writers' Project, "Charms," Folder 118c:51A.

59. Federal Writers' Project, "Charms," Folder 118c:63.

60. The Grand Zombi signifies a direct connection to the serpent religions of West Africa and the creator God, Nzambi. In addition, Li Grand Zombi can act as a blanket term for all of the snake loas of New Orleans Voudou.

61. The Louisiana Revised Statutes state that "any person who shall pretend to tell fortunes, or shall use any subtle craft, means, or device, by palmistry or otherwise, to deceive and impose upon any person, shall be deemed guilty of a misdemeanor." The law is rarely enforced, however.

See Louisiana City of New Orleans Municipal Code, Sec. 54-312 Fortunetelling. *library.municode.com.*

62. Emily Bauman, "How to Attend a Vodou Ceremony in Haiti," Visit Haiti, January 2021, *www.bing.com.*

63. Red drink refers to any red soda pop.

64. Alvarado, *The Magic of Marie Laveau.*

65. Interview with Gloria Jones, "The Wishing Spot," Federal Writers' Project, Folder 025:81.

66. Interview with Mary Washington, Hoodoo queen and card reader, Federal Writers' Project, "Marie Laveau," Washington DC: Federal Writers' Project, Folder 025:127.

67. Interview with Mrs. Josephine Jones, Federal Writers' Project, "Folklore," Washington, DC: Federal Writers' Project, Folder 025:112.

68. Interview with Lala Hopkins. Federal Writers' Project, "Marie Leveau, Her Work" Folder 025:94.

69. Interview with Joe Landry, Federal Writers' Project, "Marie Laveau," Washington, DC: Federal Writers' Project, Folder 025:57.

70. Catherine Dillon, Unpublished Voodoo Manuscript, 1939.

71. Interview with Mary Washington, Federal Writers' Project, "Marie Laveau," Washington, DC: Federal Writers' Project, Folder 025:127.

72. Federal Writers' Project, "Charms," Washington, DC: Federal Writers' Project, Folder 118c:64.

73. Interview with Mathilda Mendoza, Federal Writers' Project, "Hard Up and Broken Down," Washington, DC: Federal Writers' Project, Folder 540:4-5.

BIBLIOGRAPHY

Alvarado, Denise. *The Conjurer's Guide to St. Expedite*. Prescott Valley, AZ: Creole Moon Publications, 2014.

Alvarado, Denise. *The Magic of Marie Laveau: Embracing the Spiritual Legacy of the Voodoo Queen of New Orleans*. Newburyport, MA: Weiser Books, 2020.

Alvarado, Denise. *Voodoo Hoodoo Spellbook*. San Francisco, CA: Weiser Books, 2011.

Alvarado, Denise. *Witch Queens, Voodoo Spirits, and Hoodoo Saints: A Guide to Magical New Orleans*. Newburyport, MA: Weiser Books, 2022.

Alvarado, Denise, Carolina Dean, and Alyne Pustanio. *Hoodoo Almanac 2012*. Prescott Valley, AZ: Planet Voodoo, 2012.

Alvarado, Denise, and Madrina Angelique. *Workin' in Da Boneyard*. Prescott Valley, AZ: Creole Moon Publications, 2012.

Ball, Ann. *A Handbook of Catholic Sacramentals*. Huntington, IN: Our Sunday Visitor, 1991.

Breaux, Hazel, and Robert McKinney. Federal Writers' Project. "Hoodoo Price List." In Robert Tallant Papers, 320–321. City Archives, New Orleans Public Library.

"Conjuring and Conjure-Doctors in the Southern United States." 1896. *Journal of American Folklore* 9, no. 33 (April–June 1896): 143–147. *https://doi.org/10.2307/532980*.

Federal Writers' Project: Slave Narrative Project, Vol. 3, Florida, Anderson-Wilson (with Combined Interviews of Others). Washington: Library of Congress, 1941.

Federal Writers' Project. "Voodoo, 1937–1941." Folders 025, 118, 118A, 317, and 319.

Frazer, Mary Harris. *Kentucky Receipt Book.* Louisville, KY: Press of the Bradly & Gilbert Company, 2022.

Gamache, Henri. *The Master Book of Candle Burning.* Old Bethpage, NY: Original Publications, 1998.

"How to Conjure," *Journal of American Folklore* 12, no. 46 (1899), 229.

Hurston, Zora Neale. "Hoodoo in America." *Journal of American Folklore* 44, no. 174 (October–December 1931): 317–417. *https://doi .org/10.2307/535394.*

Hurston, Zora Neale. *Mules and Men.* New York: Harper Perennial Modern Classics, 2008. First published 1935 by J. B. Lippincott & Co. (Philadelphia).

Hyatt, Harry Middleton. *Hoodoo—Conjuration—Witchcraft—Rootwork.* Hannibal, MO: Alma Egan Hyatt Foundation, 1974.

Long, Carolyn Morrow. *A New Orleans Voudou Priestess: The Legend and Reality of Marie Laveau.* Gainesville: University Press of Florida, 2006.

The Romance of New Orleans New Orleans: Lybcus Publishing Co., 1919.

Saunders, William. "The History of Votive Candles." Catholic Education Resource Center. 2003. *catholiceducation.org.*

Saxon, Lyle, Edward Dreyer, and Robert Tallant. *Gumbo Ya-Ya: Folk Tales of Louisiana.* Gretna, LA: Pelican Publishing Company, 1987.

Speck, Frank G. "A List of Plant Curatives Obtained from the Houma Indians of Louisiana." *Primitive Man* 14, no. 4 (October 1941): 49–73. *https://doi.org/10.2307/3316460.*

Thurston, Herbert. "Candles." *The Catholic Encyclopedia* 3 New York: Robert Appleton Company, 1908. Accessed June 21, 2023. *newadvent.org.*

"The Voudou Queen." *The Worthington Advance* [Minnesota], July 7, 1881.

FURTHER RESOURCES

American Rootwork Association *americanrootworkassociation.com*
The American Rootwork Association (ARA) is a coalition of practicing root-workers, scholar-practitioners, and tradition-keepers interested in formalizing the study of Rootwork, rootdoctoring, and related folk traditions as serious areas of academic and cultural inquiry.

Conjure Corner *conjurecorner.com*
The official free educational blog and forum for Hoodoo, Conjure, Rootwork, and Witchcraft at Crossroads University.

Conjure Doctors *conjuredoctors.com*
ConjureDoctors.com is a website devoted to honoring the ancestors of the Hoodoo, Conjure, and Rootwork traditions. It provides free information about conjure doctor cures, remedies, core practices, harms and cures, household receipts, articles, resources, and an indigenous perspective on the history of Hoodoo.

Creole Moon *creolemoon.com*
The author's website promotes a spiritual lifestyle brand that features high quality artistic devotional candles, ritual oils, perfumes, sachet powders, dolls, and hard-to-find Hoodoo curios designed to promote a lifestyle filled with magick.

Crossroads University *crossroadsuniversity.com*
Crossroads University is an innovative cultural learning program developed by the author. As an online learning resource, the courses are designed to pass on indigenous knowledges that are otherwise forgotten in today's busy, technology-focused world. Crossroads University provides access to these knowledges to those who may otherwise not have such access, fills in the blanks for those that do, and helps those who wish to reconnect to their cultural roots.

Denise Alvarado *denisealvarado.com*
The official author website for Denise Alvarado.

Marie Laveaux *marie-laveax.com*
Marie-Laveaux.com provides information about the life and work of the legendary Pope of Voodoo, Marie Laveaux—a free woman of color who practically ruled New Orleans in the mid-1800s.

The Marie Laveau Voodoo Grimoire *laveauvoodoogrimoire.com*
Official website for *The Marie Laveau Voodoo Grimoire*. Find articles and information related to the content of the book, including controversial cuts, outrageous outtakes, and things too shocking to make it to print. Be sure to visit by the dark of the moon.

IMAGE CREDITS

Figure 1. African American woman and child outdoors, standing by boiling kettle of water, c. 1901, photo is in the public domain: Library of Congress image ID cph.3b11147; Wikimedia Commons.

Figure 2. The author's first book on grimoire magick, purchased when she was eleven, in 1971. Photo courtesy of the author.

Figure 3: Portrait of Betsy by François Fleischbein (1801/1803–1868), oil on canvas. This version is following restoration efforts in 2017. The Historic New Orleans Collection, call number 1985.212., Public Domain, *wikipedia.org.*

Figure 4. Conjuring image has been adapted by the author for this book. Original photo is by cottonbro studio at pexels.com and is in the public domain.

Figure 5. Ritual items in a box is by Alina Vilchenko at *pexels.com* and is in the public domain.

Figure 6. Label for magnetic lodestones designed and sold by the author on her website, Creole Moon. Image courtesy of the author.

Figure 7. The portrait of Marie Laveau by Frank Schneider (1920), based on an 1835 painting by George Catlin that has since been lost, is in the public domain: Wikimedia Commons.

Figure 8. Old praline woman image is in the public domain.

Figure 9. The calas lady photo is courtesy of the author.

Figure 10. The midwife going on a call photo is courtesy of Library of Congress, Prints & Photographs Division, Farm Security Administration/ Office of War Information.

Figure 11. The Creole cough cure ad appeared in *The Lafayette Adviser* (Lafayette, Louisiana) on February 18, 1899, page 4.

Figure 12. Photo of the author's grandmother's remedy for hoarseness courtesy of the author.

Figure 13. The burning an herb bundle photo is by Anastasia Shuraeva from pexels.com and is in the public domain.

Figure 14. The photo of Adam and Eve Conjure oil is courtesy of the author.

Figure 15. The photo of Happy Times, Amor, and Algiers Fast Luck conjure powders is courtesy of the author.

Figure 16. This rendering of Marie Laveau's house on St. Ann Street by an unknown illustrator appeared in the New Orleans *Times Picayune* on Sunday, June 22, 1890.

Figure 17. The Rose of Jericho artwork is by the author.

Figure 18. The photo of War Water is courtesy of the author.

Figure 19. The Seal of the Precious Blood image is an original design by the author.

Figure 20. The gris gris photo is by the author.

Figure 21. The money paket photo is courtesy of the author.

Figure 22. The photo of an altar for the Voudou Queen is courtesy of the author.

Figure 23. The photo of the author and her conjure dawg Zephyr is courtesy of the author.

INDEX

C

ABOUT THE AUTHOR

Denise Alvarado was born and raised in the rich Creole culture of New Orleans, Louisiana. The author of numerous books including *The Magic of Marie Laveau*, *Voodoo Hoodoo Spellbook*, and *The Voodoo Doll Spellbook*, she is a teacher of Southern Conjure at Crossroads University. Visit her at *www.creolemoon.com*.

TO OUR READERS